The Wealthy CRNA

Insights Into Becoming a Financially Successful Certified Registered Nurse Anesthetist

Jeremy L Stanley, CFP®
CRNA Financial Planning®

ISBN: 1480257451
ISBN-13: 9781480257450
Library of Congress Control Number: 2012921095
CreateSpace Independent Publishing Platform
North Charleston, South Carolina

Dedication

I dedicate this book to my loving wife Sara (who happens to be a CRNA) and to my beautiful daughter Lauren.

This program has been prior approved by the American Association of Nurse Anesthetists for 4 CE credits:
Code #1031189—Expiration Date 01/31/2016

After reading this book please go to www.crnafinancialplanning.com to access the test center.

You will be required to provide your name, address, phone, email address and AANA # in order for your test grades to be submitted to the AANA and your certificate to be mailed to you.

(Please note that you must score 80% or better to receive credit on the chapter tests, and that each test may be taken only one time.)

Table of Contents

About the Author   vii

About CRNA Financial Planning®   ix

Introduction   xi

Chapter 1
I'm Making Money- Now What!?   **1**

Chapter 2
Dealing with the Dreaded 'D' Word- Debt   **21**

Chapter 3
The Business of Freelancing and Tax Planning for CRNAs   **33**

Chapter 4
Investing 101 for the CRNA   **57**

Chapter 5
Retirement Planning for the CRNA   **71**

Chapter 6
Estate Planning Basics for the CRNA   **95**

Student Section   99

Chapter 7
Prior to Starting Anesthesia School- What to Think About   **101**

Chapter 8
I'm Finished with Anesthesia School- Now What!?   **107**

Resources   111

About the Author

Jeremy Stanley is President of CRNA Financial Planning˚. As a CERTIFIED FINANCIAL PLANNER, CFP®, Jeremy has provided financial advice and guidance to his clients for almost two decades. CRNA Financial Planning® is part of the American Association of Nurse Anesthetists' Member Advantage Program.

Jeremy has been working with the NC Association of Nurse Anesthetists for over a decade. An advocate of education, Jeremy teaches SRNAs the fundamental principles of financial management in preparing for graduation. During these classes, taught at the Nurse Anesthesia Student Programs Jeremy addresses the unique monetary challenges faced by SRNAs and outlines specific financial goals designed to help position students for financial success following graduation.

Through his work with numerous CRNA clients over the past decade as well as his participation in SRNA financial management training, Jeremy is well versed on the financial opportunities available to those in this profession. As a presenter at several annual state meetings, Jeremy imparts this wisdom to students and practicing nurse anesthetists.

As a goal driven person himself, he has a passion for helping individuals work toward their goals of financial independence. Jeremy tries to live his life by this quote from Theodore Roosevelt; "It behooves every man to remember that the work of the critic is of altogether secondary importance, and that, in the end, progress is accomplished by the man who does things." It is Jeremy's passion to help his clients ignore the critics and become financially successful.

Jeremy is a member of the Estate Planning Council, has been a Chairman's Club producer with LPL Financial for multiple years, a Member of the Wake Forest Planned Giving Advisory Council, President of the Board of Directors for CareNet Inc., is a supporter of the Susan G Komen Foundation, and has been interviewed and quoted by many media sources

About CRNA Financial Planning®

Our Mission Statement is more than just words...

To inspire CRNAs in making informed decisions through education, communication and service that exceeds their expectation.

...it's the action we take. Let me define for you what a few of the keywords in our mission statement mean to us.

Inspire -Our goal is to inspire you, our client, to live a life by design, not by default. Money is a tool to help you get the most out of your life; after all this is not "Monopoly money" it's your life savings.

Informed Decisions – Once you are inspired to share what you want out of life, we help you make informed decisions that are logical for you; bringing our resources together to develop a plan so that you can work toward your dreams.

Education –Making informed decisions can only be accomplished through education. You don't need to understand everything we do, but you do need a 10,000 foot view of what we are doing, why we are doing it, and how it applies to you.

Communication –Our communication doesn't stop at education our goal is to know you as a person and not just as an account.

You will never be disappointed in the level of communication you receive from CRNA Financial Planning®.

Service Which Exceeds Your Expectation –We aspire to deliver a level of service which will exceed your expectation. In today's world expectation of service has never been lower; so we are going in a different direction...delivering Five Star service with FedEx efficiency.

How can we do all this? Because we are independent, we do not have proprietary products, therefore we are able to provide you with unbiased advice on financial products and services that are geared to you. It means we are bifocal, paying attention to what is happening today and anticipating changes on the horizon. In addition the culture at CRNA Financial Planning® is based on an unwavering belief in integrity and fair dealings, treating our clients and each other with dignity and respect.

Introduction

Why write a book for CRNAs? Because CRNAs are unique, giving individuals. Because so many of my friends are CRNAs. Because the demands on their time demand a book on financial planning that gets to the point. This is that book.

Since a very young age I have had an interest in understanding money and finances. In fact, in elementary school I would buy a bag of candy and take it to school to sell to the other kids, always at a profit I might add! People say that wisdom comes with age and as I got older I learned that I not only understood money and planning but that I had a real passion for helping other people with their understanding of finances and how they work.

CRNAs are a very type "A" (most) driven individuals that have learned to handle stress and pressure on a daily basis. But most CRNAs have never had someone teach them about finances and what type of planning to do in order to meet their own personal goals. With over 16 years' experience working with CRNAs I have learned a lot about their understanding of money and finances which makes me uniquely qualified to write this book.

Times may be changing but some things, like having a plan, never change. My goal in writing this book is to inspire you to take some of your "much in demand" time, sit down and put a plan in place. The old saying "No one plans to fail, they just fail to plan" is more often true for the busy person than for the penniless. For some the idea of actually looking at everything in order to devise a plan is alarming – perhaps they feel that doing so will somehow limit their freedom. But the truth is that it will empower you, having a plan will give you a sense of direction and freedom; it will help you sleep well at night.

Chapter 1

I'm Making Money- Now What!?

Most people don't plan to fail financially; they simply fail to plan at all.

To reach all of your financial goals and dreams, you need to create and follow a personalized financial plan. A sound financial plan involves building a foundation. This foundation will provide the infrastructure necessary to build your financial future upon.

To begin, spend time creating a realistic household budget, evaluating your employer provided benefits and carefully considering major purchases such as a home and automobiles.

Establish a Budget

As a CRNA professional, you need to establish a working budget (the dreaded 'B' word) for your household. While the 'B' word is certainly not something that many people enjoy working on, it is an essential component to any sound financial plan.

When establishing a budget, your ultimate goal should be simple- to live below your means!

To begin, create a comprehensive list of all of your household's expenses. To aid you in this process, collect the past 3 months of your bank statements, utility statements and credit card statements.

Work through each document, organizing expenses into the categories listed below:

Fixed Expenses

- Mortgage Payment or Rent
- Property Taxes and Insurance (if applicable)
- Auto Loan(s)
- Auto Insurance
- Student Loans
- Credit Card Payments/Other Loan Payments
- Household Utilities (i.e. electric, cable, gas, water, garbage/sewage, internet and cable)
- Groceries

Your list of fixed expenses should include anything that is a recurring expenditure within your household, and that is necessary. Once you have organized this portion of your household's expenses, it is time to move onto your variable expenses (the areas that tend to get most of us into financial trouble).

Variable Expenses

- Dining Out
- Entertainment
- Gifts
- Travel
- Clothing
- Charitable Donations
- Misc (watch out for this bucket!)

Now that you have outlined all of your ongoing expenses, you need to determine what your monthly discretionary cash flow looks like.

While you can work through this process manually, there are two fantastic software tools to help you organize your finances; Quicken and Mint.com. With both platforms, you can organize your financial life into an easy to manage, online account.

Alternatively, you can calculate your discretionary cash flow the old fashioned way:

*Total Household Income- Total Household Expenses
(Sum of Fixed and Variable Expenses)
=Discretionary Income*

Fingers crossed that your discretionary income figure is positive!!

Your discretionary cash flow represents the funds available to fuel your financial goals. In the event that this figure is negative, you need to take corrective action immediately to avoid digging yourself deeper into consumer debt (which is likely occurring already as a result of ongoing spending).

Now that you have identified how much discretionary income you have available, you need to put those hard earned funds to work for you.

Max Out Your Retirement Plan

Whether you chose to work at a hospital, in a group practice, as a freelance professional, or in several capacities, you need to leverage any and all retirement plans currently available to you.

If you are currently working in a hospital, or in a group practice, then you likely have a 401(k) plan available to you. Let's take a closer look at what this type of retirement plan is, how it works, and how it could benefit you.

A 401(k) plan is a qualified plan established by an employer, enabling employees to defer a portion of their income on either a pre-tax or after-tax basis, as outlined by the plan's guidelines. In some cases, an employer may choose to match employee contributions on a percentage or dollar amount basis (i.e. 3% or 5% of the amount deferred by the employee).

Funds invested within a 401(k) plan grow on a tax deferred basis (meaning no ordinary income taxes are due annually on any investment gains). When the plan participant chooses to withdrawal funds following the defined retirement age of 59 ½, proceeds will be treated as ordinary income. If a plan participant chooses to withdrawal funds prior to their attained age of 59 ½, the funds withdrawn will be subject not only to federal income taxes, but a 10% penalty, unless the purpose of their withdrawal meets a plan defined hardship (i.e. disability).

Now, you can't contribute into the plan at any amount you choose. For 2013, plan participants can defer up to $17,500 of their earned income into their 401(k). If the plan participant is over the age of 50, the catch-up provision rule applies, enabling them to save an additional $5,500, for a total of $23,000 in 2013. Your employer will help you to establish an automatic deduction into your retirement plan from your paycheck, at your desired frequency and amount (i.e. 3% deducted on a bi-weekly basis).

Keep in mind that while maxing out your employer sponsored retirement plan is critical; saving $17,500 per year won't be enough to make your retirement goal a reality! You will need to save more.....we will discuss other investment vehicle options in Chapter 8.

In addition to kick-starting your retirement savings program, you need to take a step back to consider how you will protect your household against any unforeseen life events. While no one enjoys thinking about scenarios such as illnesses, accidents or even premature deaths, taking the time to develop a plan of action should any of these events occur is important.

Disability Insurance

Too often, CRNAs consider their homes to be their largest financial assets. And while a piece of property certainly does possess value, and is likely one of the largest, if not the largest investments you will ever make, it isn't your largest asset- YOU ARE!

What comes to mind when you think of the term 'disability'? The most common responses include car accidents or general accidents causing bodily harm. While these occurrences certainly fall into the 'disability' category, according to the Center for Disease Control, the most common causes of disability are illnesses, namely heart disease/attacks, cancer, depression, lower back injuries and complications due to pregnancy (Source: http://www.cdc.gov/Features/dsAdultDisabilityCauses/).

If you are thinking that this won't happen to you, maybe these facts will challenge your thinking:

- Approximately 1 in 4 Americans between the age of 20 and 29 will become disabled during their lifetimes. And, more than 10% of all Americans between the ages of 18 and 64 will become disabled during their lifetimes (Source: Social Security Administration, Fact Sheet March 18, 2011).
- There are currently 36 million Americans currently classified as disabled (Source: U.S. Census Bureau).

Consider what would happen in the event that you weren't able to earn an income-

- Would your household have enough additional income sources to cover basic needs in the event that you weren't able to return to work?
- If you have children, would you have enough income to cover their expenses in addition to continuing their college savings plan?
- What would happen to your current retirement savings program? Would you be able to continue to save at the necessary levels?

The answer to most of these questions is a resounding 'NO'. While families might be able to maintain their household's basic living expenses either through a company provided disability program and/or through spending down their cash reserves, they often do not have sufficient resources to cover variable expenses or to continue their current level of savings. The result- debt accumulation!

Disability Story – Sandy

A year before I injured my back, I had become an independent financial planner and investment advisor. Fortunately, I had the insight to know how important DI coverage was—so I bought my own policy after losing my employer's group provided coverage, just 6 months before the onset of my disability.

When I bought my policy, I trusted the guidance of my advisor at Disability Specialists (DSI) and I am so very grateful for my faith in the company and their knowledge & professionalism. The only regret I have is not getting the inflation rider AND maximizing my monthly benefit. Like many, I thought it was unimaginable that I would ever need any DI benefit, and if I did, it would be a short lived situation.

That's what we all tell ourselves anyway. It's been three years now and I'm still not back to work.

When I secured my policy, my primary concern was making sure our mortgage & utilities were covered—and "since it would never happen to me", I really didn't think I needed more coverage than that. At the time, I was very active and was the epitome of good health. I had just updated my life insurance benefits and received the best health rating possible. My only concern when applying for disability coverage was my list of extracurricular activities, because they potentially put me at risk for an injury. Oddly enough, I don't have a great motorcycle wreck or tale of tragedy to tell—I simply stepped in a snow bank when hiking and something went awry; the pain was instant and excruciating. These are the silly stories I hear from others at physical therapy—over & over... people just like me without an impressive "catastrophe", resulting in their becoming disabled.

Around the same time, I also developed an auto-immune disease, rheumatoid arthritis. It is uncertain if this resulted from the injury and consequent stress on my system, or if it contributed to the injury. Regardless, the injury will heal; the autoimmune disease will not. I am so very thankful I have my DI and life policies in force, as now, I am deemed uninsurable by virtually all insurance companies. It's so hard to believe that within just 6 months of getting my disability policy and being in perfect health, I became not only uninsurable, but totally disabled.

As a result of my experience, I want to share my learnings with others:

1) *Disability really can happen to anyone. As I have struggled through this journey and through physical*

therapy, I have seen people of all ages (literally from 2 up!), struggling with injuries or illness that randomly struck. Disability is an equal opportunity beast; it does not care who you are, how active you are, or that everything in your life is going your way.

2) *Buy as much as you can with all the bells and whistles. I didn't have enough DI coverage. The one thing I underestimated was the cost of being ill or injured despite having very good medical insurance coverage. It has been financially devastating and without the DI, we would have been living with relatives and lost every single asset (home, vehicles, motorcycles, investments, etc.) along with our sense of pride.*

3) *Buy an individual disability policy; do not rely solely on employer provided Group Disability coverage!!*

Disability Specialist is not affiliated with or endorsed by, LPL Financial or CRNA Financial Planning®

Disability income insurance serves as income replacement for the underlying insured party. It is designed to replace a portion of the insured's income in the event that they are unable to work due to an illness or injury.

Let's discuss the two primary types of disability coverage available to you:

- **Group Disability Coverage**

Group disability insurance may be offered by your hospital or group practice. If so, be sure to enroll!

A few things to keep in mind about your group disability insurance:

- Group disability insurance benefits are often limited/capped at 60% of your gross salary, up to $10,000 per month.
- If your group insurance premiums are paid using pre-tax dollars, the benefit received will be taxed as ordinary income in the event of a disability. YES....taxed!! This means that if you were to become disabled, you would receive approximately 40% of your current gross monthly income to live on.
- Nervous and mental issues, including depression, are often not covered.
- Most group disability insurance doesn't offer financial protection for income earned outside of the hospital or group practice (i.e. freelance income), or any overtime income earned above and beyond your base salary.

In order to fully understand how your group disability insurance program works, and what benefits are provided or not covered, read your insurance policy's certificate. In addition, keep in mind that coverage offered through your group's plan isn't generally enough to cover your household's financial needs. In this event, it is important to consider adding individual disability insurance coverage to your financial portfolio.

- **Individual Disability Coverage**

Individual disability insurance coverage can be purchased in addition to the benefits offered via your employer's group plan.

One of the biggest advantages to an individual disability insurance policy is that because premiums are paid on an after-tax basis, the benefit received in the event of a disability is treated on a tax-free basis. Another significant benefit is that the policy is portable. Should you choose to change hospitals, practices or even to work as a freelance CRNA, the coverage secured in your individual disability policy will remain in-force, providing ongoing financial protection for your household regardless of where your career may take you.

The level of coverage selected should be based on the financial gap between what you need and what your group plan provides. In addition to selecting the basic benefit level, you will have a variety of customization options available to you, including:

- Waiting Period (30, 60, 90, 120 days)
- Payment Terms (i.e. 5 years, to age 65)
- Optional Riders

Through the CRNA Financial Planning® process, you will be able to determine how much additional disability insurance is required beyond your group plan's benefits, and what specific plan features should be included in an individual policy to meet your financial needs.

While we are on the topic of insurance, let's discuss the other possible worst case scenario and its possible impact to your family- premature death.

Life Insurance

Insurance protects what matters most to you!

Life insurance can help shield those that you love from financial consequences resulting from your premature death.

Before we dive into examining your life insurance needs, let's take a closer look at the impact proper protection can have on the loved ones left behind.

Client Case Study- Mary and Mark

Mary, a CRNA, and her husband Mark, a 39-year-old computer technician, were in the process of buying a home. They both owned a small life insurance policy. But Mary, knowing the hardships that could befall a family, was determined to obtain additional protection.

They wanted to drop their current coverage and purchase two larger life insurance policies. Their advisor encouraged them not to get rid of the old policies, and certainly not until the new ones were in effect

A couple years later, Mark was on his way to the office and a tractor trailer hit him on the highway and he passed away. Mary was devastated and wasn't able to concentrate on anything through her grief. She and Mark were living somewhat comfortably on both of their salaries but had stretched beyond their means. She had two children and not enough money in reserves to take care of the existing bills not to mention continuing their savings for college.

The advisor was a friend of the family and knew within a day about his death. He ordered the paperwork to start processing the claim immediately. He let Mary know that he would take care of this for her and reassured her that everything was going to be alright financially. They had completed a needs analysis with their advisor which determined that they had a $1.0 million dollar need for life insurance. He would be delivering the check to Mary very soon.

Today, Mary and the kids are back on their feet, the kids are all taken care of for college and Mary doesn't have to worry about the bills. She is so thankful for life insurance.

How much life insurance do you need? Well, the answer to that question is 'it depends'.

To begin, assess your specific life insurance coverage needs by:

1) Evaluating your current household's ongoing expenses
2) Considering your current financial obligations (mortgage, auto loans, student loans, consumer loans)
3) Calculating how much life insurance coverage you currently have (individually owned policies and group programs offered through your hospital or practice)
4) Calculating your survivor's (spouse and children) income needs. This figure should represent how much income is

required to cover their expenses over the duration of their lifetime.

5) Evaluating any other basic survivor needs (college education for your children, retirement, or any other personal goals you have defined for your household)

Taking the time to consider each of the above scenarios will help you work to determine how much life insurance is sufficient for your personal requirements. If you don't have the desire or patience to work through the steps outlined below, a simple answer to the question of how much life insurance you need to protect your household is 5-10 times your annual salary.

For example, if you are currently earning $120,000 per year as a CRNA, you should carry between $600,000 and $1,200,000 in total life insurance face value.

Whether you choose to look at a more precise calculation of how much life insurance you need, or you opt for the quick version, the bottom line is that you need to seek coverage to protect your loved ones in the event of your premature death.

Once you have determined how much life insurance you need, it is time to move on to selecting the type of policy that best matches your given situation.

There are two primary types of life insurance: term insurance and permanent insurance.

Term Insurance

Term insurance provides protection over a pre-determined time period (or term). For example, 1 year, 5 years, 10 years, 15 years, 20 years or even 30 years. The insured party will pay an annual premium over the selected term period. Should the insured pass away during the term period, the designated beneficiaries will receive the policy's proceeds. Should the insured pass away after the term period elapses, the designated beneficiaries would not receive any policy proceeds. Term insurance policies do not build cash value.

Term insurance is generally the least expensive option!

Permanent Insurance

Permanent insurance policies (whole life, universal life and variable universal life) are designed to provide financial protection for the lifetime of the insured party. As long as the insured party continues to pay the policy's premiums, the designated beneficiaries will receive the policy's death benefit upon the insured's death. These types of insurance policies can build cash value, which could be utilized during the lifetime of the insured. If you are currently maxing out your annual retirement plan contributions, then saving into a permanent life insurance policy may be an option worth considering.

For most people, life insurance is meant to take care of their loved ones in the event of a premature death. With proper planning, once retirement age is attained, there should be little need for life insurance, as an income stream should be available to cover basic household expenditures.

Now that we have covered some of the what-if financial scenarios, let's move onto some more fun topics. As a CRNA professional, you are likely considering some significant purchases and whether if they make sense to tackle now, or whether you should wait.

Buying a House

You may be considering one of the largest purchases you will ever make- buying a home. If so, you are probably wondering if you can afford to buy a home, what the process entails and how much mortgage you can afford.

Keep in mind, that 'only fools rush in' to buying a home! Take the time to work through the process, educating yourself along the way, so that you not only end up with the house of your dreams, but that the house fits within your overall financial plan.

How Much House Can You Afford?

Before you even get to the point of searching for a piece of property, you need to assess how much capital you have available for a down payment and what monthly mortgage payment you can afford.

The standard down payment goal is 20% of the purchase price. While you can obtain a variety of mortgages with less than 20% down, there are some distinct advantages to waiting until you have a more sizable down payment before purchasing a home.

Going to the closing table with 20% or more of the home's purchase price as a down payment can help you to accomplish two very important things- it can help you negotiate a better mortgage rate with your lender, and you can bypass paying for PMI (private mortgage insurance).

During the mortgage application process, lenders will evaluate your ability to repay the loan. The primary financial ratio assessed by lenders is your debt to income ratio. Ideally, lenders like to see that your mortgage debt to income ratio is less than 28%; your total debt to income ratio should be lower than 36% (this total debt ratio includes all consumer debts- student loans, auto loans, credit cards, and personal loans).

For example:

If your current household income is $100,000 per year, your total monthly housing expense should be less than $2,333 ($28,000 per year\12 months). The $2,333 figure should include your monthly mortgage payment, annual real estate taxes, PMI and homeowner's insurance. However, if you currently pay ongoing debt payments, these amounts must be factored into your overall debt to income ratio, thereby lowering the amount lenders will be willing to offer you for the purchase of a home. In this example, you could carry as much as $665 per month in other consumer debt payments to qualify for an ongoing mortgage payment of $2,333. If your others debt payments exceed $665 per month, the amount a mortgage lender will be willing to offer you will be reduced.

Now that you have gained a better understanding of how to determine what you can afford, it is time to start the home buying process.

Follow these simple steps to home ownership:

1) Choose the Best Mortgage for YOUR Situation

With so many mortgage options available today, it is important that you select the one that best matches your financial situation and personal risk tolerance.

Fixed Rate Mortgages- Fixed rate mortgages offer borrowers a guaranteed interest rate over the life of the loan (i.e. 15 years or 30 years). Consider fixed rate mortgages if you plan to stay in the property over the long term, if you believe that interest rates may rise in the short term, or if you are uncomfortable with the probability that your rate may increase over time.

Adjustable Rate Mortgages (ARMs)-ARMs offer a fixed mortgage rate for a specified period of time, but can adjust up or down following that guaranteed period. For example, a 7 year ARM will offer borrowers a fixed rate over the course of the initial 7 year period, but can increase or decrease based on market conditions in the 8th year of the loan. Consider ARMs if you plan to be in your home for a short period of time, if you are willing to tolerate some interest rate risk, or if you believe mortgage rates will decline.

In addition to these two basic mortgage types, you may also be presented with interest-only mortgages, hybrids (blend between conventional and ARM loans) or even balloon loans (where a sizable balance is due at the end of the loan). Before selecting a mortgage type, be sure to speak with a financial professional about your budget, needs and risk tolerance.

2) *Get Preapproved for a Home Loan*

Before you head out shopping for a home, it is wise to take a prequalification letter with you in hand. A prequalification letter will not only help you narrow down properties within a specific price range, but once you locate a property, you can act quickly, placing an offer with some teeth (sellers are more likely to accept an offer with a prequalification letter).

Obtaining a prequalification letter involves shopping around for lenders. During this process, work to obtain several loan quotes, comparing the interest rates and closing costs of each quote. Once you select a lender, and you have an accepted offer in hand, it is time to begin the preapproval process which involves submitting financial documentation for review. A prequalification letter doesn't involve a thorough review of your finances; it involves only a quick review of few financial factors, generally giving only the initial green light to begin your search for properties.

During the preapproval phase, you will need to gather a variety of documents together to submit to the lender for final approval, including:

- Paycheck stubs
- Tax returns (generally 2-3 years)
- W2 statements
- Bank and investment statements (of particular importance will be proof of where your down payment funds are being held)

The lender will review all of the documentation provided, rendering their final opinion about the loan you have applied for. Organizing these documents in advance will help to expedite the loan approval process.

3) Close your Mortgage Loan

Once you gain final approval on your home mortgage loan and have completed all of the other steps involved in the closing process, such as an appraisal, inspection and final price negotiation, you are set to close. A closing date will generally be scheduled at a nearby title company. At this date, a variety of paperwork will be reviewed and signed, where upon completion; the seller will hand over the keys to the property to you as the buyer.

CONGRATS- *You are now a Home Owner!*

Should I Lease or Purchase a Car?

Next to purchasing a home, purchasing or leasing a car is often high up on the list of sizable purchases you will make during your lifetime. When adding a car in your household, it is important to evaluate whether it makes better financial sense to buy or lease.

Leases

When leasing a vehicle, you are essentially 'renting' over a pre-determined number of months. You are paying a specific amount on an ongoing basis for use of the vehicle. Lease advantages include lower out of pocket costs for maintenance, ongoing payments are often lower than purchasing and you can get a new vehicle every couple of years (which appeals to many consumers). For business owners (like freelancing CRNAs), lease payments are often considered a deductible expense for tax purposes, ultimately reducing the tax payer's modified adjusted gross income (MAGI).

One drawback to leasing is that you aren't building equity; you will never own the car. And, many leases contain mileage restrictions. Should you go over the allowed mileage as stated in the contract, you will be required to pay upon completion of the lease (the amount can be sizeable).

Buying a Car

Buying a car involves obtaining an auto loan. Auto loans will offer a stated interest rate, resulting in a specified ongoing monthly payment amount which is often higher than the lease rate on an identical vehicle. When you buy a car, you own an asset upon loan payoff, unlike leasing. In addition, you aren't locked into any specific ownership period; you can sell your vehicle at any point. For freelancing

CRNAs, the mileage accumulated while commuting to and from jobs may be tax deductible, which is of course, a huge financial benefit….every deduction counts!

Whether you should buy or lease a vehicle will depend upon your financial situation and whether you are working as a freelance CRNA or in a traditional setting.

Develop a Comprehensive Financial Plan

Last, but certainly not least, work through the process of developing a personalized financial plan for your household. A financial plan will involve evaluating your entire financial picture; cash flow, cash position, financial goals, retirement planning, insurance protection, estate planning, tax planning, and more. Working with a CERTIFIED FINANCIAL PLANNER® through the planning process will result in not only a clear picture of where you are today financially, but what steps you need to take to reach your defined financial goals and objectives. In addition to developing the initial plan, you will schedule regular check-points where your progress will be evaluated. As your life changes, so will your financial plan. In a nut shell, working through the financial planning process will improve your opportunity of achieving success in all aspects of your financial life.

As a CRNA, working through the steps outlined above will, for a large part, set the course for your financial future. Spend time now, rather than later, building a solid financial foundation which you can build upon as your professional career progresses.

Chapter 2

Dealing with the Dreaded 'D' Word- Debt

Going to school to become a certified registered nurse anesthetist isn't cheap. According to All CRNA Schools, (www.all-crna-schools.com) tuition will run you anywhere from as low as $10,000 to more than $110,000, depending on the school, its ranking and the state (although you can get free tuition if you enroll in active duty military service).

In addition to student loan debt, many CRNAs accumulate credit card debt, personal loans, car loans and even a home mortgage before, during or after their program's years. While leveraging debt can result in positive outcomes, improper management of it can cause your financial situation to snowball out of control! Unfortunately for a lot of CRNAs, the more you make, the more you spend.

That means, you have to carefully plan out your budget – or face a mountain of debt – both during and after you finish anesthesia school.

Let's discuss the differences between good and bad debt, strategies for managing debt on an ongoing basis, and tips for eliminating consumer debt all together.

Good Debt. Vs. Bad Debt

Unfortunately, debt is unavoidable for most people. So if you've had to borrow to pay for anesthesia school, consider ways to get more bang for your buck. How much will the interest from a loan cost you over the long haul versus investing the money? Borrowing might be the better option if you can obtain a higher return from investing as opposed to paying interest on a loan.

And believe it or not, there is a difference between good and bad debt. Bad debt occurs when you purchase items that you neither need nor can afford, such as that new big screen, high definition television you've been eyeing.

Some examples of good debt include:

- **CRNA School, Paying for Your Kids' College:** Whether you're footing the bill for your anesthesia education, or your child's college, paying for an education is categorized as good debt because the result adds value. Try to avoid borrowing against your retirement fund or liquidating your assets. Rather than dipping into your retirement fund, apply for financial aid (retirement savings do not count as an available asset). And you don't want to borrow against your home to pay tuition, because in the event of a financial emergency you could lose your home. Save as much as you can, and if you have to, apply for student loans and financial aid.

- **Buying A New Home:** When possible, strive to put at least 20% down on any home purchase in order to lower your ongoing monthly payment amount. In addition to your down payment, you also need to consider your monthly debt to income ratio, as we discussed earlier. This ratio describes the percentage of your monthly income that will be dedicated toward total debt payments; credit cards, auto loans, student loans and/or mortgages. Strive for a debt-to-income ratio between 20% and 35% when considering a home purchase.

- **Buying A Vehicle:** Unlike a house, if you can pay for a vehicle outright, then that's your best option. But most people don't have that much cash reserves. Instead, if you want/need a new car every three or four years and don't want a 10% down payment, then leasing is probably the way to go. Otherwise, put down as much as you can without hurting your financial stability, especially if you plan on driving that car after you've paid off the loan.

On the flip side, consumer debts such as credit cards, personal loans and lines of credit can be detrimental to your financial future; that is, if they are used for the wrong reasons such as the result of being unable to live within your household's means.

If you have landed yourself in any sort of debt, good or bad, it is time to learn how to tackle it!

Managing Personal Credit- Tackling those Pesky Credit Cards

There's no quicker way to accumulate mounds of debt than through credit cards!

According to CreditCards.com, the average American household carries close to $16,000 in credit card debt, while overall, the total U.S. revolving debt in May 2011 was nearly $800 billion – with 98% of that coming from consumer credit card debt.

Regrettably, many people pay their minimum credit card balances on a month to month basis, giving little thought to what the financial result will be in the long run. Unfortunately, paying only the minimum monthly payments will place you into a position whereby you may never fully repay these debts!

Consider these suggestions to help get you back on track with your credit card debts:

- **Less Is More:** Try to limit the number of credit cards you use. It will help you keep better track of your money and force better spending habits.
- **Are You Sure You Need A Credit Card?** Most people need at least one credit card – and not just for emergencies and large purchases, but to help build their credit score, too. But if you're the type who has trouble managing money and/or spend too much money, then having even one credit card could get you into major financial trouble. If that's you, then a pre-paid credit card may be a wise choice, because it still gives you some financial flexibility.
- **Pay Your Entire Balance Every Month:** It's best to pay your full amount every month. If that's not possible, pay as much as you can without hurting your financial flexibility. Remember, that's how credit card debt creeps up – by not paying off the full amount each time. And above all, don't be late with your payments.
- **Annual Fees:** Check carefully your annual fees any time you're applying for a credit card – especially if it's a premium card (platinum, for example). Those cards often charge a higher annual fee, so if you're not going to use the premium card's other benefits; it's probably not worth it.
- **Check the Actual Due Date:** Avoid unnecessary late payments and increased interest charges by paying your credit cards on or before the actual due dates.

Now that you have several proven credit card management tips under your belt, less discuss how to manage your consumer debt at large, as well as how to reduce and eliminate it all together.

At-Large Strategies for Tackling Debt

In addition to managing credit card debt, mastering general debt management tips will work to place you into a more positive financial situation overall.

Here are eight strategies for getting rid of debt.

1) **Avoid Accumulating Additional Debt:** Most Americans have some debt, usually for auto, home and school loans. But if you're trying to get rid of your debt – or at least put a sizeable dent in it – then you need to think twice about adding more debt to it. That might mean holding off on that big family European vacation until you can truly afford it.

2) **Pay In Cash, And Be Careful With Your Credit Cards:** Billionaire Mark Cuban has advice for when it comes to managing your finances: Get rid of your credit cards, and pay in cash whenever possible. While you'll probably still need at least one credit card to pay for major bills (mortgage, auto, school loans), paying in cash will keep you disciplined.

3) **Save, Save, Save!** Save as much money as you possibly can. It's easier than you think, too. Instead of grabbing a burger and fries from the local fast food joint, bring your lunch to work. Instead of driving to work, take the bus or ride your bike. Give up the sodas and coffee for water. You will be surprised how much you can save by making small lifestyle adjustments- most changes you won't even miss!

4) **Create A Budget:** This is one of the most important debt management steps!! Create a list of all your recurring bills (auto insurance and loan, mortgage/rent, utilities, cell phone, groceries, etc.). When you subtract this figure from your monthly income, you will know how much is available for savings, emergencies and extra things, such as dining and entertainment. To help manage your personal financial situation, considering turning to tools such as Quicken or Mint.com, both which offer online software management platforms that are simple and easy to manage.

5) **Look for Savings:** You can find savings just about anywhere. If you're buying groceries, start clipping coupons and buy generic brands. If you've got a credit card or cards, call around to see if anyone can lower your interest rate or offer you special interest on a balance transfer, then consolidate your loans onto the credit card(s) with the best interest rate(s). Shop around for a better cell phone plan. See if you can lower your cable bills by shopping around for a different satellite provider. Move into a smaller, more-affordable place – or move closer to work to reduce travel costs (i.e. gasoline and wear and tear on your automobile).

6) **Avoid Fees:** If you're late making a payment, you could wind up paying at least twice the amount of the original fee. But the same goes for things like taking out money from an ATM machine that's not affiliated with your bank – you'll wind up paying a fee for that, too.

7) **Automatic Deductions:** Set up your bills so that they are automatically deducted from either your credit card or your checking account. That way, you'll never be late. And if automatic deduction isn't an option set up an electronic

scheduler so that you'll never forget to make all payments on time.

8) **Consider Consolidation Loans-** In some cases; it may be beneficial to pay off consumer debts using a consolidation loan. This type of loan was designed to offer consumers a loan with a lower interest rate than their current debt obligations. Once the loan is approved, the consumer's outstanding debts will be paid in full, leaving one single payment per month left to manage. While these loans can be effective in terms of reducing interest paid, they are most useful to disciplined consumers, as the worst thing that could happen would be to pay down all of your consumer debts with a consolidation loan, only to rack up credit card balances again due to uncontrolled spending habits.

While the above tips will enable you to manage your consumer debts on an ongoing basis, you need to take proactive steps to reduce and eliminate your debts altogether.

Debt Emergence-2 Proven Strategies for Debt Elimination

To live a debt-free lifestyle involves implementing one of the following debt elimination plans: the snowball effect or the debt avalanche.

1) **The Snowball Effect:** The Snowball Effect, otherwise known to my CRNA clients as debt EMERGENCE, is the process from which you pay off your debt by starting from the lowest outstanding balance, then work your way up to the highest. First, decide how much additional money you can pay every month toward your debts. Next, compile a list of your

debts, starting from lowest to highest balances. Then, pay the minimum on all of your debts, but increase your payments toward the lowest debt balance first. Once you've paid off the smallest bill, add that payment toward your next lowest balance, while maintaining your minimum payments across all other debts. Repeat this cycle until all of your debts have been repaid in full.

2) **Debt Avalanche:** This strategy works in opposite fashion to the debt snowfall effect. With debt avalanche, you pay off your highest interest debts before moving on to the ones with low interest rates. To start, determine how much additional money you can pay each month toward your debts. Next, list your debts from highest to lowest interest rates. Then, pay the minimum toward each account, increasing the payment toward the highest interest account until it's paid off in full. Once you have paid off your first account, transfer this payment amount onto your next highest interest rate account for the next payment cycle. You will continue this process until your debts have been repaid in their entirety.

Client Story:

Here is a story of debt elimination in action. Mary & John wanted to know when they could retire; but, the real question was 'IF' they could retire.

You see, this couple met and married while still in college, living off student loans, which is typical for many young couples. However, upon graduation, they entered the 'real world' loaded down with debt. Debt soon became their lifestyle. In fact, they eventually couldn't remember a time that they actually paid cash for anything. They owed over $250,000, more than half of which was credit card debt. Despite of this situation, they wanted to retire in only 10 years.

Now along the way, this couple did manage to make several smart choices; they bought life insurance policies and they were currently maxing out their retirement plans. Despite their good behaviors, heading into retirement with the amount of debt they had amassed was just not feasible.

In order to address the situation, they began by listing all of their debt balances, interest rates (most of the rates on the credit cards were over 20%) and the monthly payments in order to see the whole picture in a single spreadsheet. They then calculated the interest paid on the total debt if they were to continue making their current payments (which were higher than the minimum). The interest alone amounted to almost $80,000 and would take almost 10 years to payoff, provided they did not charge any more to their respective cards. Seeing everything on one spreadsheet was like shock therapy, putting them into a "need to change" mindset.

Now that they were in the right state of mind, they began with a debt reduction strategy, which including re-financing their mortgage (both the first and the second,) reducing their average interest rate from 8% to 4.75% over 15 years, and ultimately the payment by a whopping $386 month. In addition, they were able to pull out equity from their home in order to pay off their largest credit card balances.

They then applied for less expensive term insurance, thereby reducing monthly expenditures while maintaining the needed level of death benefit. They were then able to use the cash value from one of their older life insurance policies to make a large dent in their revolving credit card debt.

Using the monthly payment amount they had been paying, they set up a debt reduction schedule to pay off all remaining debt within 4 years.

The hardest part of the strategy was wrapping their heads around the idea that they could pay cash; but with the refinance of the house, they now had an extra $386 month in discretionary cash flow.

This financial plan was put into action several years ago, and while the repayment schedule has not been applied every month (things do pop up occasionally that throw any solid financial plan off kilter), they are now closer than ever to becoming debt free prior to their retirement. Becoming debt free will mean that they will have $6,000 per month in expenses that they will not be obligated to pay during their retirement, giving them a tremendous amount of financial flexibility.

Having a solid financial plan in place helped them to see where they were, where they wanted to be, and how to get there.

Now that we have tackled some of the basics for managing, reducing and even eliminating your debt, there is likely one last question lingering on your mind left to answer; and that is, should your goal be to pay off your home mortgage early?

Should My Goal Be To Pay Off My Home?

Regardless of your household's annual earnings, getting out of debt can be challenging – especially if you've taken out loans to complete anesthesia school. If one of your financial goals is to pay off your mortgage early, there are a few things to take into consideration.

- **The Pros of Paying Off Early:** Paying your mortgage off early can save you thousands, if not hundreds of thousands of dollars in interest.

  For example, if you take out a $500,000 home mortgage with an interest rate of 3%, the interest you would save if you repaid the loan in 15 years versus 30 years is approximately $137,364.

  If repaying your mortgage in 15 years seems a bit too ambitious, try paying bi-weekly as opposed to monthly. Following a bi-weekly repayment plan can shorten your mortgage's term by nearly 7 years! Essentially, you are paying an extra mortgage payment every year.
  Last but not least, paying down your mortgage early will give you additional disposable income to spend on the things you enjoy!

- **The Pros of Staying the Course:** By staying the course, you will to continue getting tax deductions and potentially real estate tax deductions on your annual federal return.

- **Will Paying my Mortgage Off Early Improve My Credit Score?** You can, indeed, improve your credit score by paying off your home early, but not by as much as you would think.

  For example, a person with a credit score of 630 and is paying off a $250,000 mortgage should expect to improve his or her score by only 5 to 10 points. The reason? Your mortgage is what's called an installment debt.

  The same goes for paying for your car loan early. Installment debts are just what they sound like: debts paid for in installments. The reason they don't have a major impact on your credit score is because borrowers (you) typically pay these types of loans before paying off their credit cards. And, unlike credit card debt, the amount of the loan compared to your remaining balance doesn't have as great of an impact on your score simply because it typically takes years to pay off installment loans, plus there's little reduction in principal for several years.

Debt is a critical obstacle for many CRNAs to overcome, as student and auto loans, mortgage payments and other financial obligations can start to pile up during and following anesthesia school. The keys to getting out of debt are commitment, developing a strategic financial plan, and patience. If you stay on top of your finances or get help from a CERTIFIED FINANCIAL PLANNER®, you too, can eventually life a debt-free lifestyle.

Chapter 3

The Business of Freelancing and Tax Planning for CRNAs

Have you ever wanted to be your own boss? You could set your own schedule and pick and choose your assignments. The more you work; the more money you earn. Need a vacation? Tired of hospital politics? All of this is now under your control.

That's why working as a freelance CRNA is so appealing. As a freelance CRNA, you're essentially operating as a small business owner. But with that comes insurance and tax responsibilities that are normally handled by an employer

Picking the Right Business Model

You don't want to wind up paying more than you 'should' in federal income taxes, nor do you want to be hit with an unpleasant surprise when it comes time to file your taxes. That's why, as a freelance CRNA, your first step should be to consider how you should structure your business.

The three most common types of CRNA business structures are sole proprietorships, limited liability corporations (LLC) and S Corporations.

- **Sole proprietorship:** In a sole proprietorship, the onus is on you. Legally, there's no distinction between you and your business, and all profits and losses are passed on to your individual tax return. In other words, you're held responsible for anything that happens while running your "business," and you have little legal protection. For example, if a patient's vocal chords are inadvertently traumatized during intubation, and the patient then decides to file a lawsuit against you, you could be liable for any financial damages if the court rules in the patient's favor. But, generally speaking, tax accounting is much simpler as a sole proprietorship (you typically need to fill out the one-page Schedule C tax form, which is like a profit and loss statement). And it's relatively easy to upgrade to an LLC when, and if, circumstances warrant the change.

- **Limited Liability Corporation:** You and your personal assets are legally protected with a limited liability corporation, or LLC. Unlike a sole proprietorship, an LLC is a real business. That means, the business is held responsible for anything that happens, not the individual owner of the LLC. So, using the same above example, your personal assets would be protected from any lawsuit filed against the business. When it comes to your tax returns, the LLC's income is passed along to your individual tax return, and you're not subjected to self-employment taxes. Your insurance (i.e. health insurance) can be deducted as a business expense, too. But setting up an LLC is best if it's done with an attorney or accountant who specializes in freelancers. Otherwise, something may fall through the cracks.

- **S Corporation-** An S Corporation enables corporate income, losses and deductions to pass through to the shareholders for tax purposes. Individual shareholders of S Corporations report the flow-through of income and/or losses on their personal tax returns, taxed at their respective tax rates. One of the largest benefits to this corporate structure is the ability to avoid double taxation associated with C Corporation structures.

Once you choose the business structure that best suits your needs, you need to focus on protecting yourself and your business from malpractice lawsuits.

Malpractice Insurance: Protecting Yourself

There's good reason why CRNAs are among the most handsomely compensated types of nurses. Simply put, there are any number of things that could go awry while administering anesthesia. Even the most veteran CRNAs need some form of protection due to the professional risks involved, which is why malpractice insurance is a necessary evil. And it's not cheap, either. Malpractice insurance can cost anywhere from $2,000 on up to $10,000-plus per year, depending on the types of cases you work on.

The insurance will cover all expenses related to defending you against a malpractice claim, including attorney fees and indemnity payments. There are two types of insurance companies: admitted and non-admitted. With an admitted company, your policy is approved by your respective state insurance regulator, the policy forms are approved and rates have already been established. With non-admitted insurers, the opposite is true. Non-admitted companies are for those persons who have been denied by admitted companies.

Professional liability and Specialty Risks coverage are among those that admitted carries will often not underwrite. But because non-admitted carriers do not file their rates with the Department of Insurance, they can retain their ability to price risks according to

35

each specific exposure. If not for the non-admitted carrier many with high loss potential or specialty risks would be uninsurable. Regardless of whether a carrier is admitted or non-admitted, the best way to determine the security of your policy is to check the financial rating of the company. AM Best is the independent industry standard for rating insurance companies.

Although you're not under the umbrella of a doctor's malpractice insurance, freelance CRNAs have options when it comes to the cost, including medical malpractice insurance companies, local clinics or hospitals and through the American Association of Nurse Anesthetists.

- **Local clinics/hospitals:** Some local agencies, like hospitals or clinics, will pick up the tab for the cost of your malpractice insurance. This is ideal if you're typically contracted out by one or two organizations. But if you plan to work for numerous hospitals and clinics, this isn't ideal.

- **American Association of Nurse Anesthetists ():** Because malpractice insurance is often complicated, many CRNAs (including freelancers) utilize the AANA Insurance Services. And as of 2010, CRNAs can now purchase occurrence coverage. Prior to that, CRNAs could only buy claims-made coverage. With a claims-made policy, the insurer must pay the costs for a wrongful act that occurred during the policy period. But once that policy expires, you're on your own. That's why policy holders often buy a "tail," which is kind of like buying an extended warranty in that it extends your coverage period. Now, though, CRNAs can purchase occurrence coverage. With this coverage, the insurer is always required to defend the policyholder, regardless of when the wrongful act occurred. The cost differences are not significantly different.

For example, the cost for an occurrence policyholder during a five-year span would be approximately $16,500; the cost of a claims-made policy would be approximately $13,600; or about $16,800 if a "tail" is also purchased.

- **Medical Malpractice Insurers:** CRNAs can also purchase insurance through an independent company. Like any type of insurance, it's good to shop around, but be weary of picking the cheapest insurer – you might not be fully covered.

What Kind Of Health Insurance Will I Need?

Medical malpractice insurance isn't the only policy you'll need to buy as a freelancer. You'll also have to foot the bill for health, dental, life and disability insurance.

COBRA benefits are always an option if you're coming from an employer that offered group rates. A COBRA plan will temporarily extend your health coverage for up to 18 months. 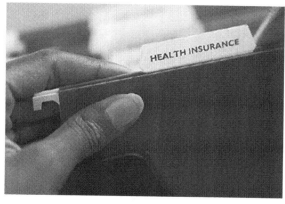 It's also typically more expensive than coverage for active employees. That's because you're paying the entire sum of the premium, as opposed to active employees, whose employer pays part of the premium. And although the U.S. Department of Labor says COBRA coverage is typically less expensive than individual health coverage, with all the options available for independent contractors, you can still buy an individual plan at a reasonable price.

Again, COBRA plans are a temporary fix. You'll eventually want to buy your own health, dental, life and disability insurance. That's when an insurance broker comes in handy.

Thanks to the Internet, shopping around for your own medical benefits has never been easier. The challenge with that, however, is the possibility of overlooking something in the fine print that jacks up your monthly premium (think optional ad-ons). You can also find a reasonably priced plan through a direct insurer, but you're not just paying for your health insurance. Direct insurers have lots of overhead and marketing costs, so you're also paying for that, too.

Instead, an insurance broker can take care of all of that – in less time and often at a lower cost. Brokers search through various insurance databases to find the most competitive rates to fit your particular needs. You're also more likely to get individual attention with independent brokers rather than dealing with numerous agents and departments. And an insurance broker should be able to negotiate lower costs for those pesky ad-ons.

In terms of workers compensation insurance, most clients won't require freelance CRNAs to provide proof of it because they're independent contractors. However, if you have any employees, you may be required to carry workers comp. An insurance broker can go over those requirements with you.

Manage Your Money, Grow Your Business with a Financial Planner

Managing your money is complicated enough. But for a freelancer? Figuring out all the deductions, the amount you should be saving for tax purposes and general record keeping can be a nightmare – even for the most veteran freelance CRNAs.

To improve your odds of achieving your financial goals, partner with a CERTIFIED FINANCIAL PLANNER® that has the experience, expertise and temperament to work with you not only today, but along your entire financial journey.

The Certified Financial Planner (CFP®) designation is universally considered to be the "Gold Standard" in the field of financial planning, portraying industry competence to individual investors. The CERTIFIED FINANCIAL PLANNER® undergoes years of studying and examination certification, similar to the education path taken to become a CRNA.

According to the Certified Financial Planning Board of Standards Inc, as of February 2012, there are 65,361 registered CFP® professionals. CRNAs are unique professionals, requiring a unique set of financial planning skill sets to achieve long term success.

Saving For the Future

Alas, you can kiss employer-sponsored retirement plans goodbye once you venture into the world of freelancing. But you still need to save for the future.

You don't have to get bogged down right away with all the various types of retirement accounts. Instead, start out by tucking away a percentage of each paycheck. This will allow you to build up a balance – which you may need if opening an investment account.

The problem with freelancing, though, is that your income is rarely the same from paycheck to paycheck – but most retirement accounts are created for people with consistent incomes. While you can do something as simple as opening a retirement account at your bank, a CFP® can help you sift through all of the retirement planning options. Remember, too, that some CFP's® work specifically with or specialize in CRNA freelancers, so be sure to ask first.

Maintaining the Proper Credentials

If you've ever worked at a hospital or clinic before, there's a good chance that you were given several reminders about continuing education, maintaining your skills, demonstrating your proficiencies and maintaining your hospital's credential requirements – whether you needed it or not. But you're on your own as a freelance CRNA when it comes time to maintaining your certification and re-certifications.

That process is overseen by the National Board of Certification and Recertification for Nurse Anesthetists, or NBCRNA. It works independent of the AANA to ensure that all CRNAs have met certification requirements that exceed benchmark anesthesia qualifications and knowledge.

Recertification takes places every two years. The two categories of recertification: full and interim.

- **Full certification:** Aside from your initial certification, you'll also need to show documentation showing your compliance with all state licensure requirements for CRNAs; documentation showing proof of 40 hours' worth of approved continuing education; and certification that shows substantial engagement in the practice of nurse anesthesia, which consists of a minimum of 850 hours over a two-year period.

- **Interim Recertification:** The two types of interim recertification are provisional and conditional. This is for CRNAs who, for whatever reason, are not in full compliance with all of the NBCRNAs' recertification requirements. Provisional recertification is typically for those who haven't substantially engaged in the practice of nurse anesthesia; a conditional recertification may be handed out on the condition that the respective CRNA enroll in and attend a drug or alcohol rehabilitation program.

The NBCRNA can verify the credentialing status of a freelance CRNA. Otherwise, many hospitals and clinics use a medical staffing agency or healthcare recruiting firm to verify those credentials.

Where Do I Find Freelance Work?

By now, you've established a business model, secured insurance and the proper credentialing, and you have found someone to help manage your money. Now comes the biggest step: Finding freelance CRNA jobs. Based on the market outlook, it shouldn't be difficult to find work.

According to the American Association of Nurse Anesthetists, there are more than 36,000 CRNAs in the United States, administering about 27 million anesthetics each year. And CRNAs are the sole anesthesia providers in close to 10% of all health care facilities and about two-thirds of all rural facilities. The average salary? About $140,000 per year.

Aside from the risks and responsibilities, the high salary can also be attributed to the shortage of CRNAs. Simply put, there are more jobs than available candidates. According to a U.S. Department and Health and Human Services report, there is a nurse anesthetist shortage of more than 5,000 across the nation. In other words, the freelance jobs are out there, you just need to know where to look. Here are a few tips when hunting for your next freelance CRNA assignment:

- **Staffing agencies:** Whether you're looking for locum tenens, permanent placement or freelance work, there are several staffing agencies nationwide that specialize in CRNAs. These agencies will know of openings in all types of settings, too, from large urban hospitals, private practice plastic surgeons, out-patient surgical centers and even small, rural hospitals or clinics.

- **Physician offices:** According to the latest statistics by the U.S. Bureau of Labor Statistics, physician offices will see the most employment growth for CRNAs because more procedures are now available in outpatient centers, physician offices and ambulatory care centers. The growth rate for CRNAs in physician offices is 48%, followed by home health care services (33%), nursing care facilities (25%), employment services (24%) and public and private hospitals (17%).

- **Social networking:** You can do much of the job search yourself from home, as most facilities that administer anesthesia services will also post openings online. But if you're looking for freelance work, you should also take advantage of social media sites like LinkedIn. Essentially, LinkedIn is an online business networking site. There, you can search directly for jobs, but you can also find and network with others in your industry. More and more employers are using LinkedIn, too, as a recruiting tool.

How to Negotiate a Contract

The amount of money you'll receive depends on factors like location, type of assignment and experience. When it comes time to discuss a contract, let the prospective client start the negotiation, which gives you leverage. If the two of you are far apart, see if you can negotiate other perks, like money upfront or a guarantee of future assignments. If you intend to work at one or two particular facilities, you may be able to work on a retainer basis, which will guarantee you a steady income. Remember, the goal here is to work out a deal that's mutually beneficial.

Why Should I Consider Freelance Work?

Working as a freelance CRNA offers significant benefits; including financial and lifestyle.

Freelance employment offers the ability for a CRNA to earn additional revenues outside of their current hospital or group practice employment. For retirees, freelance employment enables CRNAs to keep their toe in the game, working as desired when opportunities present themselves for additional income, or just for fun.

In terms of lifestyle, freelance employment offers flexibility. As a freelance CRNA, you can work virtually anywhere, anytime, with proper state licensing (and some facilities will even pay your travel and accommodation fees). In addition, you retain control over your work schedule. Remember the mad dash to turn in your holiday requests? You no longer have to worry about that as a freelancer. If you don't want to work, for whatever reason, or just want to work part time, all of that is within your control.

And you can cherry-pick your assignments. Which hospitals pay the best? What clinics have the best facilities? Who needs the most help?

While working as a freelance CRNA comes with a whole new set of responsibilities, it can also be a very rewarding career choice.

Taxes! Taxes! Taxes!

If you are like most professionals, the word 'tax' is simply overwhelming; income taxes, sales tax, property tax, estate tax, etc. etc......the list of taxes assessed can seem never ending. If you are freelancing, you are eligible to deduct business expenses that wouldn't be available to someone who is working for a hospital.

If you are working freelance as a CRNA, you may be eligible to deduct relevant business expenses in addition to non-reimbursed expenses paid while working in your hospital position. Eligible business expenses include costs that are deemed ordinary and necessary for the operation of the underlying business. As a freelance CRNA professional, you may be able to deduct some or all of the following business expenses:

o   Business travel
o   Use of your vehicle for business purposes (car payment/lease payment, repairs, mileage, gas, maintenance)
o   Business meals and entertainment
o   Continuing education, particularly that required to maintain professional licensing requirements
o   Supplies and tools required for your position
o   Capital expenses such as start up costs or business assets
o   Business use of your home- Typically, this refers a home office and any costs resulting from use of that home office (utilities, phone lines, cable, and internet).
o   Business insurance- Some examples could include business liability and personal disability insurance premiums

As with any deductions mentioned, you MUST keep adequate and accurate records of any and all business expenses. Don't worry; it isn't as hard as it sounds to track expenses. Simple receipts and notations will suffice.

According to a 2009 study performed by The Tax Foundation, nearly 56% of all Americans feel that their taxes are too high. As a CRNA professional, you fall into the

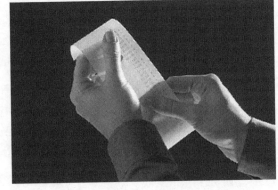

category of 'high earners'. Therefore, you are probably more tuned in than most to the concept of taxes, as the more you earn, the more you seem to pay!

There is good news for CRNA professionals!

By utilizing many, or all, of the tax management strategies outlined below, you can gain better control of your annual tax bill.

Tax Filing Tips

As you prepare to file your federal income taxes annually, keep in mind that there are a variety of tips available for reducing your adjusted gross income (AGI), thereby reducing the amount of taxes owed.

1) Use the Correct Filing Status

Your filing status determines your filing requirements, standard deduction amount, eligibility for a variety of tax deductions and the amount of tax owed annually. Currently, there are five IRS filing statuses; Single, Married filing Jointly, Married filing Separately, Head of Household, Qualifying Widow with Dependent Child(ren). It is important that you select the correct filing status for your given situation.

Here are a few <u>IRS provided tips</u> for helping to determine which filing status is most appropriate for you:

o   Your status on the last day of the year determines your status for the entire year. For example, if you were married on December 27th, even though you spent the majority of the year working as a single professional, you must file your return as married.

o   If more than one of the available filing statuses is applicable, choose the one that results in the least amount of tax owed.

o   If your spouse died during the tax year, and you didn't remarry, you may choose to file a joint return for that respective tax year.

o   Married couples can choose to file separate returns, but depending upon their state of residence, a financial benefit may not result.

o   The term 'head of household' applies to filers who are not currently married. In order to claim this filing status, the individual must be financially responsible for at least 50% of all costs resulting from maintaining a household, including those costs of another qualifying person.

2) Deduct Eligible Charitable Contributions

Annual gifts to qualified charitable organizations may be deemed an eligible itemized deduction. Each gift must be noted on Schedule A of your 1040. If your annual cash

gifts are in excess of $500, you must also complete IRS form 8323, which must be attached to your completed return. If you received benefits as a result of your charitable donation, only the amount in excess of the benefit received may be deducted. Non-cash property as well as investment donations can be deducted at their fair market value. If you donate clothing or other household items, consider using available online value calculators to determine the total value of your contribution, saving these records in the event of a tax audit. Records for all donations must be maintained; bank records, payroll deduction notices, charitable donation receipts from the qualified organization or phone records for text message donations.

(Source: http://www.irs.gov/newsroom/article/0,,id=255842,00. html)

3) Claim Eligible Tax Credits and Exemptions

According to IRS figures as reported in a 2011 Kiplinger's article, nearly 45 million Americans itemize, resulting in roughly 1 trillion in tax deductions. Missed tax deductions can be costly! (Source: http://www.kiplinger.com/features/archives/the-mostoverlooked-tax-deductions.html)

You may be eligible to take advantage of one or more of the following tax credits, exemptions or deductions:

- *Earned Income Tax Credit*- For CRNA employees who earned less than $49,078 from wages or self-employment, a tax credit up to $5,751 may be available.
- *Child and Dependent Care Tax Credit*- If you have paid ongoing expenses for the care of qualifying children, a disabled spouse or other dependent, including a parent, you may be eligible to take advantage of this credit. For more information, review IRS Publication 503.
- *Child Tax Credit*- If you have qualifying children, you may be eligible to take a deduction up to $1,000 per child in addition to the above mentioned childcare credit. For more information, review IRS Publication 972.
- *Education Credits*-These education credits are available to help offset higher education costs for yourself or eligible dependents. There are two primary education credits currently available, which include:

o *Lifetime Learning Credit*- Up to $2,000 may be deducted for each eligible student for higher education expenses such as tuition and fees, books required to complete the courses, and relevant supplies and equipment. The credit is eligible for couples married filing a joint return with modified adjusted gross incomes of $120,000 or less.

o *The American Opportunity Credit*- Up to $2,500 per eligible student may be deducted for up to 4 years of postsecondary education. Each eligible student must be pursuing either an undergraduate degree or approved credential. Full credit is available to married couples filing a joint return with modified adjusted gross incomes of $160,000 or less.

o *Home Improvement Tax Credits*- If you made energy saving home improvements to your primary property you may be eligible to take advantage of several tax incentives. You may be eligible  to receive as much as 30% of the cost of your improvements as a tax rebate, depending upon the type of improvement, the total cost and the products utilized. Some of the improvements eligible for rebate include windows, roofing, insulation, HVAC equipment and installation of energy saving technologies such as heat pumps. For a complete list of eligible products, visit the U.S. Department of Energy's website at http://energy.gov/savings.

- *Sales Tax Deduction-* While this tax offers benefits for all U.S. residents; it offers the greatest benefit for residents of states not currently imposing state taxes. Why? Filers can deduct the greater of their state and local income taxes or state and local sales taxes. If you completed large retail purchases within the most recent tax year (car, boat, furniture for your new property, etc.), then this deduction could result in significant federal income tax savings. To calculate whether this deduction could benefit you, use the <u>IRS provided calculator</u>.

4) Deduct Eligible Business Expenses

Employees as well as business owners may be eligible to deduct qualified business expenses on their annual tax returns.

In order to qualify for these employee business expenses, you must be itemizing using Schedule A. CRNAs working in traditional hospital settings, may be eligible to deduct the following non-reimbursed business expenses:

- Business travel- (airline tickets, car rentals, taxi cab fees, business meals and entertainment)
- Use of your vehicle for business purposes
- Business meals and entertainment- *(**Tax Tip:** Be sure to note who you dined with on the receipt for verification purposes when it comes time to claim the deduction)*
- Continuing education, particularly that required to maintain professional licensing requirements
- Supplies and tools required for your position

In order to deduct qualified business expenses, you must maintain records to serve as proof (bank statements, receipts, mileage logs). In addition to taking advantage of each of the credits and exemptions you may be eligible for, be sure to spend a few minutes annually reviewing your tax withholding status. If you receive either a sizable tax bill or refund annually, it may be wise to adjust your paycheck's withholdings. If you owe, you need to increase the amount taken from your paycheck in order to balance out your payments. If you receive a refund, you are essentially providing the government with an interest free loan by providing your hard earned capital over the course of the tax year. Instead, adjust your withholdings so that you receive these funds over the course of the year. Additional discretionary cash flow can be utilized for a variety of purposes, including debt re-payment; cash reserve accumulation or retirement investments.

Tax Favored Investment Strategies

In addition to taking advantage of eligible deductions and credits, tax benefits are available to investors who select particular investment strategies. Because CRNA professionals are highly compensated, tax favored investing is particularly beneficial. Let's take a look at some of the better known tax favored investment strategies and how they can benefit your financial situation.

Tax Exempt Alternatives

Municipal Bonds

Municipal bonds (or Muni's) refer to debt securities issued by states, municipalities or counties to finance capital expenditures such as construction of bridges, schools or even highways. When an investor purchases a municipal bond, they are loaning the underlying entity funds in exchange for interest payments. At the end of the defined investment period, the bonds mature and the investor's original investment is returned.

Municipal bonds provide exemption from federal income taxes, but other state and local taxes may apply. However in some cases they may be exempt. (Otherwise referred to as Triple Tax Free).

For example, a resident of Washington could receive triple tax exemption; they would be exempt from paying local, state and federal income taxes on their municipal bond's earnings.

Municipal bonds are subject to availability and change in price. They are subject to market and interest rate risk if sold prior to maturity. Bond values may decline as interest rates rise. Interest income may be subject to the alternative minimum tax.

Roth IRA

The Roth IRA is a retirement investment account whereby investors contribute funds on an after-tax basis, the capital grows on a tax-deferred basis, and if certain eligibility requirements are met, the funds can be withdrawn on a tax-free basis.

To contribute to a Roth IRA, individuals must not exceed income requirements as outlined by the IRS. For 2013, the following are eligible to participate in a Roth IRA investment account:

- o Married filers filing jointly with a Modified Adjusted Gross Income of <$178,000
- o Filers that are married filing separately, filing as head of household or who are single with a Modified Adjusted Gross Income of <$112,000

As contribution eligibility changes annually, be sure to consult the latest IRS guidelines prior to making an annual contribution into a Roth IRA investment account.

Tax Deferred Investments

"Tax deferral" describes a method of postponing the payment of income tax on currently earned investment income until the investor withdraws funds from the account. Tax deferral is encouraged by the government to stimulate long-term saving and investment, especially for retirement.

Deferring income taxes owed on earned investment income enables the principal to accumulate earnings on a compounded basis. Over time, the impact of compounding can be significant.

Let's consider a simple example of how significant the benefit of compounding interest can become over time.

> *Two investors contribute $1,000 annually over a 30 year period into 2 separate accounts. Investor A selects a tax deferred investment vehicle, while Investor B selects a taxable account.*
>
> *Assuming an average growth rate of 8% and that Investor B would be subject to the 20% capital gains tax, let's examine what their approximate resulting account balances would be.*
>
> *At the end of this 30 year period, Investor A's account balance would be nearly $70,000, while Investor B's account balance would be roughly $30,000; less than ½ of Investor A's!!*

Another benefit of tax deferral is that withdrawals from these investments often occurs at a later date, such as retirement, when the investor is subject to lower federal income tax rates.

Investors can take advantage of tax deferral benefits through investing in a variety of investment account types, including:

- *Qualified Retirement Plans*- Investors may have the option to contribute funds into qualified retirement plans on a pre-tax or after-tax basis. Funds invested within these accounts grow on a tax deferred basis, taxed as ordinary income upon withdrawal following the investor's attained age of 59 ½. Qualified retirement plan examples include 403(b)s, 401(k)s, as well as Roth and Traditional IRAs.

- *Fixed Annuities*- Annuities are investment vehicles offered by insurance companies, designed to provide income streams to the investor at a specified date. The annuity holder is taxed upon withdrawal of the funds.

Pre-Tax Qualified Plan Investing

Because CRNA professionals are highly compensated, it is critical that pre-tax investment options are taken advantage of! Pre-tax contributions into qualified retirement plans can reduce the individual's adjusted gross income for tax purposes. The most common employer provided qualified plans include 403(b)'s and 401(k)'s.

- *401(k)*-For 2013, plan participants may defer up to $17,500 of their annual earned income on a pre-tax or after-tax basis into their employer sponsored 401(k) plan. For participants over the age of 50, the IRS currently offers a catch-up provision, enabling an additional $5,500 to be contributed.
- *403(b)*-For 2013, the total of both employer and employee contributions into a 403(b) retirement plan cannot exceed the lesser of $51,000 or 100% of eligible compensation plus catch up provisions. The limit on elective deferrals made by the plan participant is the same as for a 401(k) retirement account; $17,500 for the 2013 tax year.

For CRNAs who are also working freelance, the option to contribute additional funds into a retirement program designed for the self-employed may be available. *You read correctly; you may have the option of taking advantage of multiple retirement plan options simultaneously!*

There are two primary qualified plan types available to the freelance CRNA: the solo 401(k) and the SEP IRA.

- **SEP IRA**- SEP, or simplified pension plan, refers to a qualified retirement plan designed for employers and self-employed individuals. One of the distinct advantages to working as a freelance CRNA is the ability to set up and contribute to a SEP IRA in addition to your current qualified retirement program through your primary employer. As of 2013, employers can contribute up to 25% of eligible income, up to $51,000, into a SEP IRA. These same limits apply to self-employed individuals.
- **Solo 401(k)**-Also called the Indie 401(k) and the independent 401(k), this qualified plan option offers tremendous benefits to the freelance CRNA. The annual plan contribution for this account is the same as a traditional 401(k) plan, currently set at $17,500 for the 2013 tax year. In addition, for plan participants over the age of 50, catch up contributions are permitted. The company can also contribute a profit sharing contribution of 25% of your income up to a maximum of $33,500, allowing total contributions to the plan of $51,000.

Now that you know what two plans are available is you are freelancing, you are probably wondering how to make these options work for you.

If you are working at a hospital or group practice and you are also freelancing, you have the unique opportunity of contributing to two retirement plans. Let's take a quick look at an example of how you can maximize both your employer sponsored plan and your independent plan.

A CRNA currently working with a hospital or in a group practice, can contribute up to $17,500 annually on a pre-tax basis into their 401(k) plan. If they are also working as a freelance professional, if they choose to invest into a SEP IRA account, they can contribute up to 25% of that separate income, up to $51,000 per year into their account.

For this example, let's assume the CRNA professional is earning an additional $25,000 per year working freelance. If both account contributions are maximized, the total amount saved into retirement plans for the year would be: $17,500 into the 401(k) account and $6,250 into the SEP IRA, for a total of $23,750 saved!!

As you have learned, several options are available for CRNA professionals looking to reduce their annual tax bills both today, and during retirement. At first glance, these concepts may seem a bit overwhelming. However, once you get the ball rolling, you will get the hang of things. Whether you are working for a hospital, group practice or are freelancing tax saving strategies are available for you to take advantage of.

This information is not intended to be a substitute for specific individualized tax or legal advice. We suggest that if you have any questions, you should discuss your specific situation with a qualified tax or legal advisor.

Chapter 4

Investing 101 for the CRNA

Now that you are earning a substantial income as a CRNA, it's time to get serious about something else: managing, and investing, your money. In today's volatile market, managing and investing your money is more important than ever. Simply tucking it away in a savings account may sound like the safe, sound, decision, but you won't grow your earnings. Then again, if you invest poorly or make bad financial decisions, you could pay the price for years to come.

That's because you have other financial obligations to consider, like paying off your debt, saving for retirement and possibly paying off your home. How much risk are you willing to take on? And what kind of investment vehicles are you interested in: mutual funds, stocks or bonds? As a CRNA, does your employer offer a 401k plan? Should you buy an annuity or open an IRA?

Remember, the Federal government does not insure most securities, even the ones bought through a credit union or bank that offers federally insured savings accounts. In other words, no matter what you decide to invest in, there's always going to be some risks associated with it.

Before You Get Started ...

Our disciplined investment process outlined below, illustrates the importance of several key strategies when managing your investment portfolio; portfolio review, portfolio education, defining a personalized asset allocation, implementing portfolio recommendations, and defining a core buy/sell strategy for ongoing management.

In addition to following this process, there are a number of key factors to consider under the topic of investment management, including:

- **Define your Exit Strategy:** Before committing to any investment vehicle, be sure to clearly define your exit strategy.
- **ROI and Getting Money Back:** Some investments restrict your ability to cash out your holdings. Otherwise, most other investments (bonds & stocks,) can be sold any time, although you might not get back all the money you paid for them if you pull out early. In terms of your return on investment,

bonds are considered safer because they usually offer a fixed return. By comparison, other securities fluctuate. A word of caution, though: Just because an investment did well in the past doesn't mean it will do well now.

- **How Risky Are Your Investments?** The old rule of thumb: the higher the risk, the greater the potential return – or loss. Again, most investments are not federally protected, although the federal government insures bank savings accounts; U.S. Treasury securities, including savings bonds, are also protected.

- **Reduce the Risk:** By spreading your money around in a variety of investment options, you're reducing your risks. Make sure to incorporate non-correlated assets into your investment allocation.

- **Taxes!:** Some investments have tax advantages, such as U.S. Savings Bonds, which are exempt from state and local taxes, and municipal bonds, which are exempt from federal income tax (and sometimes state income tax). You can also find tax-deferred investments that allow you to postpone – and in rare cases, eliminate – paying income taxes.

What Is Asset Allocation, And How Can It Help Me?

Although you have little to no control over how your investments will fare, there is one thing you do have control over: asset allocation. Asset allocation is an investment strategy in which you balance risks and rewards by adjusting your portfolio's assets according to your personal goals, your tolerance for risk and the market outlook. There are three primary forms of assets: cash (and equivalents), equities and fixed income. Each has its own level of risk and return and therefore they behave differently.

Determining which mix of assets to hold in your portfolio is a personal process. The asset allocation that will work best for you during the different times in your life will depend largely on your ability to tolerate risk and on your time horizon. Risk tolerance is simply the amount of risk you are willing to take to accomplish your goals. Your time horizon is the time you have until you reach that goal. A longer time frame, like saving for retirement may allow for a higher risk tolerance. While an investor saving for a teen-ager's college cost would most likely take on less risk because of the shorter time frame.

With this in mind, how can you develop your own ideal level of asset allocation? Here are seven tips:

1) **Risky Business:** The market is volatile, to put it lightly. To get started, consider bonds and fixed income investments. Generally speaking, the returns will be lower – but so, too, will the risks. You have to decide how much of your port-folio you want to allocate to things like stocks and your fixed income. When in doubt, check out some of the risk calcula-tors available online.

2) **Equities vs. CDs*:** CDs earn very little over time but carry very little risk. On the opposite end of the spectrum are indi-vidual stocks – which carry with them high risks. There are various investment options that involve risk levels that fall in the middle.

*CD's are FDIC insured and offer a fixed rate of return if held to maturity. Stock investing involves risk include loss of principal.

3) **Diversify!:** As mentioned earlier, don't load up all your investments in one investment vehicle, because if things go bad, you may lose everything.

4) **Think About Retirement:** Young investors have time on their hand and therefore can ride out any market fluctuations. But older investors need portfolio growth, too. The goal for retirement-age investors is to come up with an asset allocation that will keep them solvent for at least 30 years. Consider revising your asset allocation from time to time, regardless of your age.

5) **Old vs. New Stocks:** Established companies typically come with a history of high or stable earnings and are therefore less risky, while new companies have greater risks – but have the potential for greater rewards, too. Keep in mind, too, that smaller companies are generally riskier.

6) **Real Estate Investment Trust*:** With REITs, the profits from real estate are passed along to you, the shareholder, as a dividend. Like stocks, REITs come with risks. The REIT Company must pass on 90% of their profit in the form of a dividend to their investors, often creating an income stream for the individual shareholders.

*Investing in Real Estate Investment Trusts (REITs) involve special risks such as potential illiquidity and may not be suitable for all investors. There is no assurance that the investment objectives of this program will be attained.

7) **Understand the Importance of Sequence of Returns:** So many CRNA investors will review the historical average of returns for the investments held within their portfolios as a method of gauging how to allocate their portfolio. But, few give thought to how annual returns may impact their future retirement income streams. Historical averages can be extremely misleading to retirees! For example, if we

consider the S&P average return over the 20 year period from 1989 to 2008, the average return was 8.43%. However, it is important to note that this annual average return only applies to the investor who held these assets, not adding or withdrawing from the account, over the entire 20 year period; this isn't what actually occurs with the average investor! While the average over this period was positive, if you take a look at the first year of this sequence, the average return was -37%. And, the subsequent 9 years were also negative. While this wouldn't have affected the investor who held the assets over the entire period, these results could have been devastating to the investor who was relying upon them to produce retirement income. Understanding the potential impact of the sequence of returns illustrates the importance of putting a plan in place that is flexible and realistic for your future retirement goal.

Devise an Offensive Investment Plan

It's great to sit back and watch your money grow. But fact of that matter is; you're probably going to incur some losses, too. What would happen, then, if your investments underperform? What if you lose money? That's why you need a defensive strategy in place. You need a strategy in place that limits your risks and protects your capital, because even a small loss can require a big offensive strategy to recoup the losses.

Here are a few ways to control your losses:

1) **Don't Forget About Cash:** Consider shifting some of your capital into cash positions. You may need it someday for an emergency or investment opportunity.

2) **Trends:** Consider buying stocks that are in an uptrend; then sell them once they break that trend. Give yourself a set amount of time; if the stocks are performing poorly once you reach the end of that time frame, then it may be time to consider selling.

3) **Bet on Many Horses:** If you go to the horse track, would you put all your money on one horse? Or will you bet on several? This is the concept behind diversification, a topic already discussed. Diversification, though, will only work if the assets you buy are uncorrelated. Correlated assets display like market pricing movements whereas non-correlated assets move in opposite directions. Non-correlated assets are often included within an investment portfolio to counterbalance risk inherent in other investments.

4) **Limit Your Exposure:** Say you've been eying a relatively risky investment. You could invest a relatively small amount in it or bypass the investment altogether. Think of it this way: losing 25% on a $1,000 investment isn't nearly as painful as losing 25% on a $10,000 investment.

5) **Stop!:** With a stop-loss order through a broker, you can automatically sell all or part of your investment if it falls below a certain price. Set the price high enough that you will limit your potential capital loss.

To summarize, your overall investment strategy should include the following:

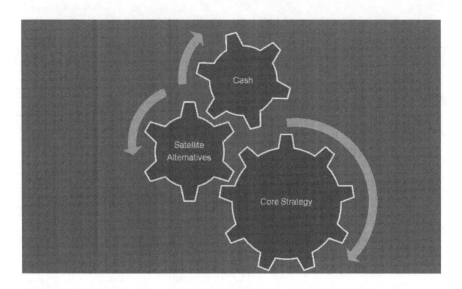

No strategy assures success or protects against loss.

Risk management matters

Managing risk is perhaps one of the most important components to investing. Simply put, you need an entry and exit plan in place. Some investors say it's even more important than making a profit. The reason? Without a careful plan in place, your opportunity for achieving financial success may not be within reach.

And while it's important to set goals, your investment plans will help you reach your financial goals. Not sure how to manage your risks? Here are eight suggestions:

1) **No Plan Is Set In Stone:** You need to have an investment strategy in place before putting your hard-earned money to work. But you also need to tweak it from time to time. Once you've got a good investment plan in place, stick with it until the market dictates changes to your portfolio. And, of course, if your plan isn't working, then it's time to devise a new one. Knowing when to change your plan is just as important.

Learn how to manage changes, follow market trends, and diversify your portfolio.

2) **Fool Me Once …:** As a CRNA, you should expect to earn in upwards of $100,000 per year– and your earnings should only go up from there. With that comes money to invest. You should expect to make a few mistakes along the way. Learn from those mistakes. If your investment plan isn't working, then it's time to consider tweaking your strategy.

3) **Get To Know Your Investments:** Learn as much as you can about your particular investments, including information about the company, past history, and the industry itself. Say you invested in a stock that came from an industry that performed well, but your stocks did not. Remember, it's easier to pick stocks for a respective industry than it is an individual stock.

4) **Stick to the Facts, And Leave Emotion Out Of It:** It's great to be optimistic, especially when you have dreams of paying off your college loans and getting rid of all your debt and retiring well. But you also have to be realistic. Take emotion out of your investments, and stick to the facts. You may have a friend or family member who steered you to a "great investment opportunity," but fact is, if you're losing money, then it's time to change directions.

5) **Know When To Cut Your Losses:** Don't try to average down your money by continuing to purchase stocks that are losing money. Instead, seek out stronger stocks that are performing better.

6) **Weigh The Pros And Cons:** Take a look at your portfolio from time to time and consider the pros and cons from each investment. This will help ensure that you are staying on track, and it can serve as an indication that you need to look at other investment vehicles.

7) **Buy and Hold**- A long term investment strategy that begins with the completion of a thorough portfolio analysis and security selection exercise. Once investment selections are in place, the investor will hold that allocation over the long term, making only slight adjustments to the assets held based upon portfolio allocation movements periodically. Investors leveraging this philosophy are not concerned with short term price fluctuations within their portfolios.

8) **Create a Personal Pension**- Utilize fixed income streams, such as personal pensions and/or social security, or a self-generated fixed income stream via an annuity, to cover your fixed costs during retirement. When you have guaranteed income sources covering your household's fixed expenses, the remainder of your portfolio can be utilized for additional income needs, inflation protection or for legacy planning.

Know Your Options ...

You have options when it comes time to investing your money. A lot of options. So many, in fact, that it's easy to get lost, confused or overwhelmed in the types of options that are available.

Generally speaking, there are two primary types of investments: Fixed income and equities.

- **Fixed income:** Types of fixed income include cash, protected securities, convertible bonds, municipal bonds, corporate bonds, government securities, treasury inflation and high-yield bonds.
- **Equities:** Types of equities include stocks, ETFs (exchange-traded funds), preferred stocks and emerging market securities.

There are alternative investment vehicles, too, such as structured notes, REITs (real estate investment trusts), managed futures, currencies and even precious metals, to name a few.

... And Consider Investing In Trends

When investing in trends, you need to pay close attention to demographic shifts, volatility and inflation. But more importantly, you need to pay close attention to the industry or industries you're interested in investing in. Of course, trends come with risks. If you were happy with how your Netflix stocks were faring in 2010, then you were probably a little disappointed when it took a tumble in 2011, with shares plummeting as much as 60%.

Do your research, above all else. But, don't fall in love with your picks! Love can hurt......

Consider investing in established names. New up-and-comers may start out with a bang before leveling out.

- **Network Security and Cyber Security:** Today's corporations must analyze, control and manage their respective networks in an effort to keep them running securely and seamlessly. And many network analytics offer security solutions, too. Likewise, cyber security is becoming increasingly important. According to a recent Federal Emergency Management Agency report, the number of reported cyber attacks in the U.S. has risen 650% since 2006, rising from 5,503 that year to 41,776 in 2010.
- **Mobile Payments:** This is still a relatively new trend, but there are a growing number of companies that offer mobile payment solutions. Market analysts say there are great opportunities for profit in the coming years through mobile payment devices.

- **Cloud Computing:** Simply put, cloud computing allows you to store digital files online. Some of the top cloud computing companies have price/earnings ratios of about 10% per year.
- **Healthcare Continues To Boom:** The healthcare industry continues to grow and is expected to represent 18.4% of the U.S. GDP in 2013.
- **Energy on a Global Scale:** Both developing and developed countries need oil to continue driving growth.
- **And, there are many, many more……**

*Because of their narrow focus, sector investing may be subject to greater volatility than investing more broadly across many sectors and companies

The Market Outlook

We keep hearing that the sluggish economy will eventually recover. And there have been positive signs pointing in that direction, too. Still, investing in today's volatile market is riskier than ever. Just how volatile is the market? Due to the country's budget deficit, the flailing housing market and the European debt crisis – among other reasons – stock valuations are at their lowest point since the early 1990s, and market volatility is at historic levels.

The average daily change in the S&P 500 since last August has been 1.7%, up or down. That's twice the daily average during the past 20 years, according to J.P. Morgan. GDP growth is forecast at 2.4% by the end of next year, and then is projected to increase to 3.4% in 2014. And the unemployment rate has been forecast at 7.7% by the end of 2013.

All of these factors make understanding both your investment and financial plan that much more important.

*The Standard & Poor's 500 Index is a capitalization weighted index of 500 stocks designed to measure performance of the broad domestic economy through changes in the aggregate market value of 500 stocks representing all major industries.

Recovering From the Recession

Part of the problem is the nation's ability – or lack thereof – to crawl out of the recent recession. In a recent report by the UCLA Anderson forecast director, the nation has yet to crawl out of the "Great Recession" of 2008-2009. In the previous 10 recessions, the GDP returned to its previous peak within two years. This recession? It could take the country seven or eight years to fully recover, according to the report. That's because a recovery needs good employment growth, something that just hasn't happened yet.

But there could be good news on the way with the housing market. According to a companion report by a UCLA Anderson senior economist, the housing market may have bottomed out already. That means, a recovery – albeit a slow one – is likely on the way. Foreclosures seemed to have peaked, and existing home sales are rising nationally. That wouldn't happen without record-low mortgage rates and a (slowly) improving labor market.

What Does All This Mean For Me?

The bottom line: Invest wisely. That, of course, is easier said than done. Diversifying your portfolio, following trends and devising a sound financial strategy will help minimize losses and, hopefully, increase your gains. And remember, whatever financial strategy you devise, take the time to reevaluate those plans on an as-needed basis. After all, the market could change drastically today. You want to make sure you're prepared for anything.

Chapter 5

Retirement Planning for the CRNA

Whether you plan to continue working as a CRNA well beyond traditional retirement age, or you plan to retire at the first possible moment you can, planning ahead will be the key to your financial success.

If you are planning ahead for your retirement, or seeking to ensure your current retirement's financial security, there are likely a number of questions lingering on your mind.

If you are **currently retired**, you may be pondering about-

- How you can make your retirement nest egg last?
- What you should do now that your portfolio's value has declined with recent market fluctuations?
- How you can generate enough ongoing income to cover your basic household living expenses?
- What are Required Minimum Distributions (RMDs) and how they will impact you?
- How will you pay for long term care costs or the rising cost of healthcare?

If you are **planning for your future retirement**, some of your questions may include:

- When can I retire?
- How much will health care cost?
- What should I be investing in?
- How can I possibly save more money than I already am? I feel tapped out.....

To answer these questions and more, you will need to walk through a number of planning steps, including:

1) Defining your Retirement Vision
2) Determining How Much You will Need to Retire
3) Assessing Your Current Financial Reality
4) Calculating Your Retirement GAP
5) Taking Action

Let's take a closer look at each of these critical steps.

Defining Your Retirement Vision

Before you can begin planning of any kind, you must clearly define where you are headed. The same is certainly true when it comes to your retirement planning. Having a retirement vision will help you define your financial goals. Plus, you are more likely to achieve your financial goals if you write them down!

To begin, let's define 'retirement' more in terms of financial independence than what many consider 'traditional retirement', as more and more CRNA professionals are redefining what this life phase looks like. Financial independence can be defined as the point in time where you have enough income and assets working for you, that working becomes optional.

Not all CRNAs will retire completely from their professions. Some will choose travel options to stay on their toes, and some may choose volunteer medical service opportunities, while others may choose to stay employed with their hospitals or group practices on a part time basis.

Before we get into the technical retirement planning lingo, spend time considering what your ideal retirement scenario looks like.

Ask yourself the following questions when working to create a personalized retirement vision:

- When do you anticipate becoming financially independent? Aka- When do you want to retire? 59 ½. 60, 65, 70, or never.
- Do you plan to retire in your current home? Downsize? Own a second home? Move to an entirely new location?
- What activities will fill your retirement days? Golf, arts & crafts, volunteering.....the list of potential activities is virtually endless!
- Are traveling plans in your future? Domestic or international? Have you created a "Bucket List" of your top travel destinations? What would best define your travel style (Motel 6 and on a budget, or all out at the Ritz Carlton)? Who do you plan on traveling with?
- Have you dreamed of starting a second career? Would you consider going back to school; whether part time or full time? Maybe you would take cooking classes, art classes, cake decorating classes or you simply want to expand your level of knowledge in a particular career or niche.

- Who do you plan to spend time with during retirement? Spouse, family, friends.....??
- How do you intend to stay healthy and physically active? Yoga, Pilates, golf, marathons, triathlons, walking, tennis, etc.
- Do you plan on spending time volunteering in your community?

Now that you have clearly defined your retirement vision, it's time to determine how much capital will be required to make it a reality.

How much will you need to retire?

To begin to answer this question, you must first define your retirement age. Your retirement age should be based upon several key factors, including:

- How much retirement capital you have or will have accumulated
- What your expected retirement expenses will be
- Your life expectancy

Once you have defined when you plan to retire, you can begin to calculate how much you will need to accumulate.

Let's take a look at some quick examples of how much you would need to accumulate to retire at various target ages:

Client 1- *Assumptions: age 40, current income $125,000 and retirement age goal of age 65. In order to achieve a retirement on par with their current lifestyle at age 65, this client would need to accumulate $4,099,000 in retirement assets assuming an aggressive growth portfolio (average rate of return of between 9–11% annually).*

Client 2- *Assumptions: age 35, current household income $140,000 and retirement age goal of 60. In order to achieve a retirement on par with this* *current household income at the age of 60, this client would need to accumulate $5,166,000 in retirement assets assuming an aggressive growth portfolio.*

If either client were less aggressive with their investments, targeting a moderately aggressive portfolio, they would need to save additional funds on an ongoing basis to compensate for the lower expected annual portfolio return.

Spending time calculating what you will need to accumulate for retirement is one of the most important activities you will participate in during the course of your financial life. Keep in mind that your financial situation will change on an ongoing basis. Therefore, it is important that you recalculate your progress annually so that any modifications to your plan can take place.

Where will your Retirement Income Come From?

Whether retirement is far away, rapidly approaching, or already upon you, it is important to understand how an income stream will be created to cover your expenses.

To keep the answer simple; your retirement income will come from 4 buckets:

- Social security
- Employer sponsored retirement plans
- Personal retirement plans and
- "Other" savings and investment programs.

Each of these income categories will be discussed further.

The Financial Planning Process- Defining What Actions Need to be Taken

Before you can begin planning for your retirement, you need to complete an assessment of where you are today financially.

The Financial Planning Process consists of the following six steps:

1. Establishing and defining the CRNA-Planner relationship.

The financial planner should clearly explain or document the services to be provided to you and define both his and your responsibilities. The planner should explain fully how he will be paid and by whom. You and the planner should agree on how long the professional relationship should last and on how decisions will be made.

2. Gathering client data, including goals.

The financial planner should ask for information about your financial situation. You and the planner should mutually define your personal and financial goals, understand your time frame for results and discuss, if relevant, how you feel about risk. The financial planner should gather all the necessary documents before giving you the advice you need.

3. Analyzing and evaluating your financial status, including your GAP.

The financial planner should analyze your information to assess your current situation and determine what you must do to meet your goals. Depending on what services you have asked for, this could include analyzing your assets, liabilities and cash flow, current insurance coverage, investments or tax strategies. And, as you prepare for your retirement, your planner will consider what GAP, if any, currently exists between your current level of assets and savings and what is required to achieve your ultimate goal.

4. Developing and presenting CRNA specific financial planning recommendations and/or alternatives.

The financial planner should offer financial planning recommendations that address your goals, based on the information you provide.

The planner should go over the recommendations with you to help you understand them so that you can make informed decisions. The planner should also listen to your concerns and revise the recommendations as appropriate.

5. Implementing the financial planning recommendations.

You and the planner should agree on how the recommendations will be carried out. The planner may carry out the recommendations or serve as your "coach," coordinating the whole process with you and other professionals such as attorneys or stockbrokers.

6. Monitoring the financial planning recommendations over the course of your CRNA career.

You and the planner should agree on who will monitor your progress towards your goals. If the planner is in charge of the process, she should report to you periodically to review your situation and adjust the recommendations, if needed, as your life changes.

Whether your retirement is deemed a financial success or not is up to you!

Now that you have defined your retirement vision, have determined how much you will need to live that vision out, calculated where you currently are in relationship to that goal, and defined your financial GAP, it is time to take some action.

What if I Am NOT On Track For Retirement?

If you have discovered through this planning process that you are not on track to achieve your retirement goal, what action steps should you consider taking to rectify the situation?

Consider the following options to put your retirement vision back on track:

- **Consider Lifestyle Changes**- If you are truly not on track to achieve your retirement goal, the most important things for you to consider implementing are expense reductions and additional savings contributions. While virtually no one enjoys budgeting, it can ensure that your retirement vision gets back on track. Work through your recent expenditures, reviewing any and all items that can be reduced or eliminated. Any discretionary cash flow that you can free up can be redirected into investment accounts earmarked for your retirement.
- **Maximize Your Employer's Qualified Plan**-For 2013, eligible employees can contribute up to $17,500 of their pre-tax income into a qualified plan such as a 401k. If the employee is over the age of 50, they can take advantage of the annual catch up provision, adding an additional $5,500 in savings into their 401k.
- **IRA Catch-Up Contributions**-For CRNAs that are over the age of 50, the option to also catch up with contributions into an IRA are available. In addition to the current annual amount of $5,500, qualified CRNAs can contribute an additional $1,000 into their IRA account.

Now that you know where you are financially and what you need to do in order to achieve your retirement goal, it is time to take action.

What are your Investment Options?

With your GAP number clearly identified, now it is time to evaluate where to invest your retirement dollars, on either a monthly or annual basis.

As previously discussed, there are three general categories of retirement investment vehicles that will contribute to your future income stream; employer sponsored plans, personal plans and everything else. Let's take a closer look at each of these categories, which investment type falls into each one and how they may benefit you.

Employer Sponsored Retirement Plans

If you are currently employed by a hospital or group practice, then you likely have access to an employer sponsored retirement plan. The two most common plan types are the 401(k) and the 403(b). Let's take a quick look at each plan, how they work and how they can benefit your approaching retirement.

401(k)

A 401(k) plan is a qualified plan established by an employer, enabling employees to defer a portion of their income on either a pre-tax or after-tax basis, as outlined by the plan's guidelines. In some cases, an employer may choose to match employee contributions on a percentage or dollar amount basis (i.e. 3% or 5% of the amount deferred by the employee).

Funds invested within a 401(k) plan grow on a tax deferred basis (meaning no capital gains taxes are due annually on any investment gains). When the plan participant chooses to withdrawal funds following the defined retirement age of 59 ½, proceeds will be treated as ordinary income. If a plan participant chooses to withdrawal funds prior to their attained age of 59 ½, the funds withdrawn will be subject not only to federal income taxes, but a 10% penalty, unless the purpose of their withdrawal meets a plan defined hardship (i.e. disability).

Now, you can't contribute into the plan at any amount you choose. For 2013, plan participants can defer up to $17,500 of their earned income into their 401(k). If the plan participant is over the age of 50, the catch-up provision rule applies, enabling them to save an additional $5,500, for a total of $23,000 in 2013. Your employer will help you to establish an automatic deduction into your retirement plan from your paycheck, at your desired frequency and amount (i.e. 3% deducted on a bi-weekly basis).

403(b)

A 403(b) works very similarly in concept to a 401(k).

As a highly compensated professional, it is strongly recommended that you contribute fully into your employer sponsored plan each and every year. Keep in mind that saving $17,500 per year into a 401(k) or 403(b) retirement plan won't be enough to secure your retirement. As a highly compensated professional, you will need to save more!

Personal Retirement Plans

Once you have maximized your employer sponsored retirement plan(s), it is time to turn your attention to personal retirement plans. Let's dive in and examine the top options, how they work and whether they fit into your financial plan.

Traditional IRA

A Traditional IRA is an individually owned retirement plan that enables qualified individuals to direct pre-tax income toward investments that grow on a tax-deferred basis. Individuals can contribute up to 100% of their earned income into the account, as long as they don't exceed the Modified Adjusted Gross Income (MAGI) limitations.

For 2013, the MAGI limitations are as follows:

Single or Head of Household	<$59,000	Full deduction up to your contribution limit
	>$59,000 but less than $68,999	Partial deduction
	>$68,999	No deduction
Married Filing Jointly	<$95,000	Full deduction up to your contribution limit
	>$95,000 but less than $114,999	Partial deduction
	>$114,999	No deduction
Married Filing Separately	<$10,000	Partial deduction
	>$10,000	No deduction

For 2013, the amount an individual can contribute into a Traditional IRA is the greater of $5,500 for filers under the age of 50, or 100% of their taxable compensation for the same calendar year. For filers over the age of 50, the current catch-up provision applies, enabling them to save the greater of $6,500, or 100% of their income for the same calendar year.

Roth IRA

A Roth IRA is an individual retirement account whereby contributions are NOT tax-deductible (like with eligible Traditional IRAs), the earnings grow tax-deferred and get this, the withdrawals (subject to IRS guidelines) are tax-exempt.

To determine if you are eligible to contribute into a Roth IRA, review the chart below.

Married Filing Jointly	<$178,000	Full amount
	≥$178,000 but <$187,999	Reduced amount
	≥$187,999	None
Married Filing Separately	<$10,000	Reduced amount
	≥$10,000	None
Single, Head of Household, Married Filing Jointly	<$112,000	Full amount
	≥$112,000 but less than<$126,999	Reduced amount
	≥$126,999	None

The same annual contribution amounts as a Traditional IRA apply to a Roth IRA, subject also to annual income limitations as outlined above.

SEP IRA

A SEP account (Simplified Employee Pension) is an IRA, subject to some of the same rules and guidelines as your Traditional IRA account.

A SEP IRA enables employers to contribute funds on behalf of their employees toward retirement, and for self-employed individuals, to make contributions on their own behalf, for their own personal benefit. One of the most important things to point out for CRNAs is that a SEP IRA can be set up in addition to an employer sponsored retirement plan, such as a 401(k) or 403(b). Why should this matter for you if you freelance? Well, this enables you to save more than $17,500 per year toward your retirement goal in a tax-deferred investment vehicle.

For 2013, eligible parties can contribute the greater of 25% of their self employed income or $51,000 into a SEP IRA. Catch up contributions do not apply for SEP IRA account holders.

Independent 401(k)

The Independent 401(k), also known as the solo 401(k) and indie k, is a retirement plan specifically designed for self-employed individuals, including freelance CRNAs.

Contributions into an independent 401(k) plan are tax-deductible, contributions grow on a tax-deferred basis, and like a traditional employer sponsored 401(k) plan; withdrawals are taxed as ordinary income. Plan contribution levels are the same as a traditional 401(k) account. However, self-employed individuals may have the option of contributing both as an employee and an employer, thus raising the total eligible contribution amount.

"Everything Else"

In addition to employer sponsored retirement plans and personal retirement plans, there are a number of other investment vehicles available to the individual investor. For more information about these investment options, refer to Chapter 8.

Whew......That was a ton of information!!

If you are currently experiencing information overload, don't despair.

If you are serious about ensuring that your ideal retirement becomes a reality, then the best step for you to take is to complete a Comprehensive Retirement Needs Analysis® (C.R.N.A.). During this process, everything that has been discussed and more will be reviewed and a personalized financial plan, including any and all necessary steps that you need to complete, will be presented for your consideration and implementation.

Retirement planning doesn't have to be overwhelming! But, it will become overwhelming if you fail to plan. To get a jumpstart on planning your retirement, fill out the questionnaire located on our website www.crnafinancialplanning.com under the Strategies for CRNAs tab.

Now that you taken the steps necessary to achieve financial independence, what's next (well, financially speaking)!?

The savings that you have worked so hard to accumulate will now become your primary source of income during retirement. To make sure that your funds will cover your needs throughout retirement, you will need a withdrawal plan. Essentially, you will need to recreate your current paycheck.

Sources of Retirement Income

To begin, let's examine where your retirement income will be sourced from.

Your retirement income will come from 3 buckets:

- Social security
- Guaranteed Income Sources
- Savings

Social Security

While social security isn't generally enough to even cover your basic household living expenses, it can certainly act as a supplement to the other income sources you have created for yourself.

Your eligibility for social security is based upon your date of birth. Currently, reduced benefits are available to qualified individuals at the age of 62, whereas full benefits become available at either age 65 or 67.

It is important to point out that just because you have attained the age of 62, 65, or even 67, doesn't mean that you MUST begin collecting social security. In fact, there could be a number of financial advantages available to your household if you delay collection. For each month that you delay receiving payments, your benefit amount increases slightly. The amount of increase is dependent upon your date of birth.

<u>If you have decided to continue working as a CRNA during retirement, whether on a part time or full time basis, then you need to pay particular attention to this</u>; *social security benefits may become taxable if you choose to continue working.*

For 2012, if you are younger than your full retirement age, $1 will be withheld for every $2 you earn above the annual earnings limit, set at $14,640. If you begin to take social security benefits during the year that you become fully eligible, you are only going to be taxed on a portion of the income earned on the side as a CRNA. For the most up-to-date information about social security, be sure to visit www.socialsecurity.gov.

Considering these social security deductions, you may decide that working during retirement as a CRNA may not make financial sense. However, as you can see, waiting until full retirement age to take social security gives you more room to earn on the side. And, if you wait until after full retirement age to work, there is currently no impact to your social security benefits. All of this said; social security may end up being only a very small portion of your overall retirement picture, so these figures may make little to no impact on your decision to keep on working during your retirement years.

Guaranteed Income Sources

If your hospital or group practice established a defined benefit pension plan in your benefit, you are among the lucky few!! A defined benefit plan, otherwise referred to as a pension program, provides a specified income stream to qualified employees upon their retirement. The benefit amount is often calculated using the employee's current age, years worked and average income over a specified period of years (i.e. last 3 years, last 5 years).

Savings

This bucket will be by-and-far your largest source of retirement income! If you have followed the advice outlined throughout this book, you will have accumulated funds in one or more of the following investment vehicles:

- Employer Sponsored Retirement Plan-401(k) or 403(b)
- Traditional or Roth IRAs
- Annuities
- Stocks
- Bonds
- Savings Accounts, Certificates of Deposit (CDs) or Money Market Accounts
- Rental Property(ies)
- Part or Full-Time Work

  o This is a unique opportunity for CRNAs. Some CRNAs love to travel and see new places. As you get older and your children become grown (not as reliant upon you financially), an opportunity exists for you to travel and still get paid A LOT! Free-lance, 1099 or travel CRNA positions exist across the continental United States. To locate these opportunities, consider leveraging staffing services or searching on job placement platforms such as www.gaswork.com. You can take an assignment for a month, or for 6 months, in your chosen geographic locations. With these opportunities, you can keep your skill sets sharp, see the country, and earn a substantial income in the process.

Your retirement income will be derived from one or all of the above sources; social security, pension plans, savings and/or part time freelance income.

Planning to Take Withdrawals-How Long will my Money Last?

The answer to this question isn't as straight forward as most people would prefer, as it depends on a variety of factors; market return, investment allocation, withdrawal rates. In addition, retirement account distributions should be done with care to avoid unnecessary penalties.

Before we dive into your withdrawal plan, let's briefly consider some important age-based retirement milestones.

62 Years Old- You can begin receiving reduced social security (if you choose to)

64 Years +8 months Old- You become Medicare eligible

65-67 Years Old- You can begin receiving full social security benefits

70 ½ Years Old- Required Minimum Distributions kick in

These important age-based milestones may or may not impact your decision of when you should retire.

For many CRNAs, the concept of retiring can seem overwhelming, particularly with recent market volatility, portfolio declines and the idea of no longer receiving a paycheck. However, with the 4% rule, calculating how long your retirement withdrawals will last doesn't have to seem like an impossible task.

The 4% Rule

The 4% rule is an easy to understand starting point for your retirement funds withdrawal strategy. Using this concept, you can create a reliable stream of income coupled with social security during retirement by simply taking 4% of your retirement savings dollar figure in income annually.

Let's say a CRNA has $1 million accumulated within their retirement portfolio. Based upon the 4% rule, she would be able to withdrawal $40,000 per year in income from this portfolio. It is important to note that this 4% rule assumption doesn't factor in the eroding nature of inflation (how goods and services become more expensive over time). Throughout my career, I have always been taught to build in inflation increases into any financial plan. However, 16 years of real life experience also comes into play where this is concerned. We have a lot of clients that have been retired for some time, and most of them become accustomed to living on a fixed income. They don't come to me each year asking for an inflation raise! Based upon our client experiences (and we have spoken to our clients about this), we typically build in a 2% inflation assumption into our client's plans for calculation purposes. This allows for those times when big expenses pop up for our clients; they will have the excess income as needed to cover these costs.

Betty a CRNA had been practicing for 30 years and accumulated $900,000 for her retirement goal. Her husband was already retired and receiving $2,800 per month in the form of a retirement pension in addition to his social security income stream of $1,800 per month. They had minimal household expenses and their mortgage was completely paid off.

First they would need to determine what was required per month to maintain their current lifestyle. Let's say for example that they needed $8,500 per month in income to maintain their current lifestyle. This meant that they would need to generate an additional $3,900 in income from their retirement portfolio. They decided that based upon the 4% rule (they would withdrawal 4% of her retirement accounts per year $900,000x4%=$36,000), she could generate an additional $3,000 per month from her investments. In addition, she would be eligible to receive social security which was estimated to be $2,000 per month, when combined with the $3,000 in income from her portfolio; she would able to reach the desired level of household income. In fact, she would be generating income in excess of their ongoing needs.

Despite the fact that they had achieved their retirement goal, she chose to work part time for a short time until she was mentally ready to step into retirement. Now, she is having the time of her life as a retiree.

Income Generation Options for Retiring CRNAs

The ultimate goal of a CRNA during retirement is to successfully generate ongoing income from their available sources; social security, pensions, and/or personal retirement savings. The pattern in which retirees withdrawal funds will be based upon their retirement age, recent market performance, income requirements and legacy planning goals.

To further explain, let's further define account types that may be available to you during retirement:

- *Ordinary:* Accounts whereby gains are treated as ordinary income; bank accounts, CDs and corporate bonds.
- *Dividend:* Accounts positioned to pay ongoing dividends subject to a maximum tax rate of 15% under the current 2012 income tax laws.
- *Appreciated:* Assets that have appreciated since they were acquired and thus will be subject to capital gains taxes upon liquidation.
- *Municipal:* Bonds that are exempt from federal income taxes; typically issued by states and municipalities.
- *Pre-Tax Assets:* Retirement accounts such as 401k's or IRA's. Upon withdrawal, these assets will be subject to ordinary income taxes after the age of 59 ½. Assets that are withdrawn prior to the age of 59 ½ may be subject to a 10% penalty.
- *After-Tax Deferred:* After tax contributions that have been made to qualified retirement accounts (401k, 403b), non-qualified annuities or non-deductible IRAs will be treated as ordinary income upon withdrawal of the assets.
- *Roth IRA and Roth 401k:* Assets that have been held greater than 5 years and are withdrawn after the account owner is 59 ½ or older will not be subject to income taxes, otherwise considered as tax-free withdrawals in retirement.

Now that we have identified the common retirement account types, let's take a look at some of the common liquidation patterns of CRNAs with differing goals. The account types are listed in order of liquidation priority.

- *Early Retirees (Prior to the age of 59 ½):* Ordinary, dividend, appreciated, municipal, Roth (up to the contribution amount), after-tax deferred, pre-tax, remaining Roth account balances
- *Retirees Focused on Tax-Minimization Strategies:* Ordinary, dividend, municipal, Roth, appreciated, after-tax deferred, pre-tax
- *Retirees Focused on Generating a Tax Advantaged Estate for their Heirs:* Pre-tax, after-tax deferred, ordinary, dividend, municipal, appreciated, Roth
- *General Retirees:* For those focused primarily on generating income throughout the remainder of their lives, the general liquidation pattern is as follows: ordinary, dividend, municipal, Roth, after-tax deferred, pre-tax, appreciated

Armed with the above information, you can navigate your way toward your retirement goal with confidence. And once you get there, you will have the tools necessary to generate an income stream that will outlive you. While much of this you may be able to accomplish on your own, many successful CRNAs choose to partner with the experience and expertise of CERTIFIED FINANCIAL PLANNER® professionals. After all, would you intubate yourself? With the right financial professional at your side, your chances of achieving your financial goals increase exponentially.

Client Case Study- We all love a success story, and I am no different!

The couple I am about to tell you about are in their 40's, and like most couples they had big dreams of an early retirement. They began by reviewing their assets and liabilities, in order to gain a realistic picture of where they were financially. They had been contributing to their retirement plans for many years, but had greatly reduced their contribution levels while paying for their 2 children's college expenses. They also had a mortgage, car payments and several credit cards eating up a significant portion of their ongoing monthly cash flow. Although their assets far outweighed their liabilities, at the rates they were spending and saving, early retirement was merely a dream. Without significant changes, they weren't going to be able to achieve their long range financial goals.

Their first homework assignment was to determine where they were spending money. They both had good jobs, but somehow there was just nothing left over at the end of each month. Once they could see where the money was being spent, they were able to redirect their spending. Their early retirement goal was a strong motivator. When they began to eat out less and stop much of their impulse buying, they found the discretionary cash flow necessary to begin building additional retirement assets.

Now that discretionary cash flow was found, they set up a debt reduction strategy. The also refinanced their mortgage to free up additional cash flow. A systematic payoff schedule for their debts, including a 15 year payment plan for the mortgage, was established, giving them a clear pathway for debt elimination prior to their dream retirement age.

They both began to contribute the maximum amount to their company retirement plans. Their advisor partnered with them, helping them design an asset allocation strategy and providing ongoing monitoring of the funds held within each of their qualified plans. In addition to their company retirement plans, using the money that had been previously directed to college payments, they opened a joint brokerage account and made monthly contributions; this was in addition to the saving account they had set up at the bank.

With any solid financial plan, it is important to address both the future and the what–if's that could derail the future from becoming a reality. One of the biggest threats to an individual's retirement is the rising cost of health care. To address this, they purchased LTC policies while in their early 50's, which enabled them to pay their premiums in full within a short 10 year period.

While they had planned for the expected and unexpected in their financial world, something unexpected happened; the death of a father left them with a small inheritance. As a result of careful financial planning and monitoring, this inheritance enabled them to retire before age 60, as they focused the funds on debt elimination.

We believe that a customized plan faithfully executed will open you up to greater success than a life lived without a plan. It is true what is frequently said…."no one plans to fail, they just fail to plan".

Chapter 6

Basic Estate Planning Concepts for the CRNA

Estate planning refers to ensuring for the orderly distribution of the property and assets within an individual's estate when they die. It is never too early to define your estate plan.

While no one enjoys thinking about their final wishes, building an estate plan is part of the financial planning process. Outlining your wishes in writing not only enables you to state what is to become of your estate, but to take the burden out of the hands of your family and loved ones upon your death. A basic estate plan encompasses a variety of documents, including a basic will, durable power of attorney, medical directive and living will.

There are several primary reasons why individuals should consider organizing an estate plan, including:

- An estate plan works to reduce confusion about what the final wishes were of an individual regarding a funeral service and/or the distribution of remains

- Ensuring that there is a chosen guardian for any children within the household that are under the age of majority within the state
- Ensuring that an individual's assets are distributed to the individuals or organizations intended
- The minimization of final expenses and taxes
- Preservation of wealth for future generations

If an individual passes away without a will, the state will determine who inherits the assets as well as will appoint a guardian for any children under the age of majority within the state. Individuals may select a simple will to protect their estate or they may require additional asset protection offered in the form of a complex estate plan, which can often include trusts and tax planning strategies for the protection of the estate.

Basic Estate Planning Terms

When learning about basic estate planning, there are several terms that you should familiarize yourself with, including:

Estate- An individual's estate includes all property and assets that were owned by the deceased prior to their distribution. An estate also includes any liabilities of the deceased.

Property- Property within an estate is typically separated into 2 categories; real property and personal assets. Real property includes the primary residence, rental or investment properties, other permanent structures, and land. Personal assets include automobiles, household furnishings, jewelry and art work, intellectual property (patents, copyrights), liabilities, bank accounts, insurance policy proceeds, investment accounts, retirement accounts and any ongoing annuity or pension payments.

Grantor- The grantor is the individual that is transferring property to another individual, often within a trust that was created within a will.

Beneficiary- This refers to the individual or individuals who are listed to receive proceeds from the grantor. Beneficiaries can be listed on individual financial accounts and insurance policies and/or listed within the grantor's will individually.

Trustee- Whoever was designated to administer the property on behalf of beneficiaries is referred to as the trustee. A trustee has a fiduciary responsibility to act in the best financial interest of those beneficiaries that they have been charged with monitoring. This information is often listed within the grantor's trust.

Successor Trustee- This individual is listed as a secondary option to act as trustee in the event that the primary trustee is unable to fulfill their duties.

Probate- The legal process of distributing assets to heirs as well as of transferring property is referred to as probate. However, there are some assets that are not required to pass through the probate process, going directly to the designated heirs or beneficiaries upon death of the property owner.

Estate Transfer- This refers to the legal process of transferring assets from the grantor to another individual.

Now that you have a better working knowledge of some basic estate planning terms, let's take a closer look at basic estate planning documents:

- **Basic Will**- defines how your assets will be distributed, who will administer your estate, who will look after your minor children (guardians) and your final wishes (i.e. burial/cremation arrangements, funeral). A will also helps your estate avoid intestacy, the process by which the state decides how and to whom your estate will be distributed.

  o **Durable Power of Attorney**- Document that allows an individual to give the authority to make financial decisions to another individual on their behalf. For example, if someone were to become hospitalized and unable to tend to their household affairs, a durable power of attorney grants the authority for someone to write checks, take care of household issues and tend to general financial affairs as needed. In general, it is advised to list a primary and secondary power of attorney.

- **Living Will**- This document defines the individual's wishes as it relates to life support.
- **Medical Directive (Health Care Proxy)**-This document grants authority to a named individual to make medical decisions on the behalf of another. Typically, treatment decisions, surgical decisions and basic medical decisions can be made by the named individual in the event that the grantor is unable to do so.

Completing the basic estate planning process is simple and easy. And, it is a critical component to any sound financial plan. Be sure to make creating your estate plan a top priority, if you have not already done so.

Student Section

Chapter 7

Prior to Starting Anesthesia School- What to Think About

SO, you are pondering about taking your nursing career to the next level by pursuing anesthesia school- CONGRATULATIONS!

CRNAs are among the highest paid nursing professionals within the U.S., earning an average annual salary of nearly $160,000, according to the American Association of Nurse Anesthetists.

Before you start anesthesia school, there are a number of things to consider- namely, how to overcome the financial and time commitments associated with pursuing this challenging, yet rewarding career path.

Anesthesia School- The Financial Commitment

One of the largest obstacles facing your chosen career path is the financial commitment. In addition to developing a plan to cover the actual cost of attending anesthesia school, you must manage to stay afloat while you obtain your certification.

As you consider where to attend anesthesia school, one of the primary determining factors will often be the program's cost. Currently, you have 112 accredited programs to select from among.

In-state tuition ranges from $15,000 to $70,000, while out-of-state tuition ranges from $20,000 to $120,000. Each school's estimated costs often include tuition, AANA membership fees, certification fees, clinical costs, and required textbooks. Supplies, such as a laptop computer, as well as living expenses, are not included.

In addition to considering the cost of attending a school's program, you must also consider how you will pay for your household's expenses throughout your enrollment period. During your time in anesthesia school, you will not be permitted to work. Are you prepared to give up 24-30 months of income?

With the cost of attending anesthesia school now at the top of your mind, let's discuss available options to help you stay afloat during your enrollment period.

How to Stay Afloat Financially During Anesthesia School

Before enrolling in anesthesia school, you must address both how you will cover the cost of enrollment and your household's expenses while you complete your coursework.

Save your Tuition Costs in Advance

If you are willing to delay enrollment in anesthesia school, consider travel nursing for a few years to accumulate the funds necessary for enrollment in anesthesia school. According to career sites such as StudentDoc.com and MedicalCareer.com, travel nurses in 2011 earned as much as $50,000 to $100,000 per year. Saving in advance for anesthesia school will enable you to avoid common debt accumulation, for either your program's tuition, or to keep your household afloat. If travel nursing doesn't fit your personal circumstances, consider leveraging available financial aid and scholarship options coupled with disciplined household budgeting to pay for your program's costs.

Leveraging Financial Aid and Scholarships

A variety of financial aid options are available for the taking during anesthesia school. Be sure to consider any and all available options, as you certainly wouldn't want to leave free money on the table.

- *AANA Scholarships*
- *Graduate School Loans*- Compare both private and federally funded loan options. Contact your anesthesia school's financial aid department for information about applications and available options.
- *CRNA Program Stipends*- Some hospitals offer stipends to anesthesia school students when they sign a commitment letter stating that they agree to work for their organization over a specified period following graduation.
- *State Association Scholarships*
- *Uncle Sam*-Joining the military offers financial assistance upon completion of a specified service term, appealing to some CRNA candidates.
- *Individual School Programs*- Once enrolled, be sure to consider any financial aid programs your anesthesia school offers to students. Opportunities may be available based on financial need, while others on merit.

Household Budgeting 101

The last thing that you want to face during anesthesia school is mounting consumer debts resulting from improper household budgeting. To avoid this outcome, spend time planning a realistic household budget to follow during your time in anesthesia school.

To begin, create a comprehensive list of all of your household's expenses. To aid you in this process, collect the past 3 months of your bank statements, utility statements and credit card statements.

Work through each document, organizing expenses into the categories listed below:

Fixed Expenses

- Mortgage Payment or Rent
- Property Taxes and Insurance (if applicable)
- Auto Loan(s)
- Auto Insurance
- Student Loans
- Credit Card Payments/Other Loan Payments
- Household Utilities (i.e. electric, cable, gas, water, garbage/ sewage, internet and cable)
- Groceries

Your list of fixed expenses should include anything that is a recurring expenditure within your household, and that is necessary. Once you have organized this portion of your household's expenses, it is time to move onto your variable expenses (the areas that tend to get most of us into financial trouble).

Variable Expenses
- Dining Out
- Entertainment
- Gifts
- Travel
- Clothing
- Charitable Donations
- Misc (watch out for this bucket!)

Once you have identified what you are currently spending on a monthly basis, you need to ensure that this figure is less than or equal to your monthly income. If not, this is the time to make budget adjustments. Once you have created a realistic budget, you must put it into action. This involves tracking on a weekly or monthly basis. In the event that your expenses are creeping past your income, you must make some adjustments (aka sacrifices) in order to stay on track.

In addition to overcoming financial obstacles associated with enrolling in anesthesia school, it is important to understand and address the associated time commitment.

Anesthesia School- The Time Commitment

As with any worthwhile career path, there is a time commitment involved in becoming a CRNA. Due to the demands placed on anesthesia students, it is important to understand that your available time outside of school will be extremely limited.

There are numerous rigors to the program including study preparation required to pass 2 exams per week. Clinical exams pose yet another challenge- you must understand and be able to explain to instructors what you are doing and why.

If you are married or have children, it is important that you discuss the demands of anesthesia school (both in terms of time and financial) so that realistic expectations can be established. While the program can be challenging, with support and strong time management skills, successful graduation can be achieved. Planning ahead will make the transition into anesthesia school easier on your wallet and your relationships!

Chapter 8

I'm Finished with Anesthesia School- Now What?

Whew; you have endured the many stresses associated with anesthesia school and have come out the other side victorious!

Now that you have completed your anesthesia program, it's time to begin the search for your perfect position. Not only should you consider what your ideal working environment looks like, but your salary expectations and benefits must have's. And last but not least, once you complete anesthesia school, it is time to focus on passing your boards so that you can become a Certified Registered Nurse Anesthetist!

Considering your Next Career Move

One of the greatest things about working as a nurse anesthetist is that you have a number of options available; hospitals, doctor owned groups, CRNA owned groups and even freelancing.

Hospitals

Doctor Owned Groups

CRNA Owned Groups

Freelancing

How to Make Heads or Tails of your Offers

Ok, so the salary portions of the offers you are receiving are straight forward. But, how can you tell which benefits packages pack any punch? What exactly should you be looking for in terms of company benefits?

As you compare and contrast offers for employment, consider the following:

- *Employer Sponsored Retirement Plans*- What type of plan is offered? Is there a company match? If so, what amount of percentage annually (i.e. 100% up to 3%)? Is there a vesting schedule on any company matches received? If so, how long before you vest?
- *Disability Insurance*- Is it offered? Is the premium 100% employer paid? What is the benefit offered (i.e. 60% up to $10,000 per month in income)? Waiting period? Is additional coverage available for purchase beyond the basic benefit?
- *Vacation Policy*- How many weeks per year will you get off? Is it paid or unpaid?
- *Education Funds*- Are funds available for continuing education courses? Additional certifications or specialties?

To simplify the benefits comparison process, develop an evaluation system. Create a priority list of the benefits that are must have's as well as those perks which while aren't deal breakers, would be nice to have. Use your evaluation process as you consider each offer for employment received. In no time, you will be able to identify the opportunity that is the best match for you and your family.

You've Passed your Boards!! Go out and Celebrate....

BEFORE you begin work as a CRNA, you must successfully complete the national certification examination which is administered either by the Council on Certification of Nurse Anesthetists or its predecessor.

After years of sacrifice and hard work, you have not only completed your anesthesia program, you passed your boards.

Reward yourself with a vacation, much needed time off, that item that you have had your eye on for some time; anything that is meaningful to you!

It's time to celebrate! **<u>Just don't go TOO crazy!!</u>**

Resources

Survey of U.S. Attitudes on Taxes, Government Spending and Wealth Distribution, Tax Foundation, 2009

www.irs.gov

http://www.kiplinger.com/features/archives/the-mostoverlooked-tax-deductions3.html?kipad_id=x

http://energy.gov/savings

http://www.irs.gov/newsroom/article/0,,id=105098,00.html

http://www.irs.gov/businesses/small/article/0,,id=109807,00.html

http://www.irs.gov/retirement/article/0,,id=111419,00.html

http://www.cdc.gov/Features/dsAdultDisabilityCauses/

The opinions discussed in this material are for general information only and are not intended to provide specific advice or recommendations for any individual. To determine which investment(s) may be appropriate for you, consult your financial advisor prior to investing. All performance reference is historical and is no guarantee of future results. All indices are unmanaged and may not be invested into directly.

Securities and Advisory Services offered through LPL Financial, a Registered Investment Advisor. Member FINRA/SIPC.

Made in the USA
Lexington, KY
09 January 2016